A TIME FOR WAR,
A TIME FOR PEACE

DEDICATION

For Francis: For our faith, our hope and our love,
the foundation of our family

A TIME FOR WAR,
A TIME FOR PEACE

by

JOAN I. SMITH

First Published in 1996 by
Dr Francis G. Smith
36 Vincent Street
NEDLANDS 6009
WESTERN AUSTRALIA

National Library of Australia Cataloguing-in-Publication entry
Smith, Joan I. (Joan Isabel), 1918-
    A time for war, a time for peace

    ISBN   0 9587538 7 3

    1. Smith, Joan I. (Joan Isabel), 1918-. 2. Smith, Francis G.
    (Francis Godfrey). 3. Great Britain. Army. Auxiliary
    Territorial Service - Biography. 4. World War, 1939-1945 -
    Personal narratives, British. I. Title.

940.548141092

Design and typeset by F.G. Smith

Printed by
Format Press
NEDLANDS WA 6009

CONTENTS

PHOTOGRAPHS

EDITOR'S PREFACE

This is the story of love and marriage of Francis Smith and Joan Bardwell told against the background of World War II and the post-war struggle to find a home, start a family, to obtain qualifications for a peace time career and, for Joan, the difficulty of adjusting from her life in the army, where she was part of a team using her brain at full stretch, to life as a house wife and mother.

Soon after they met in early 1939, when Francis was a bank clerk, he joined the Surrey Yeomanry and on 1st September of that year was mobilised for full time service in the Royal Artillery which involved him for the next six and a half years.

Soon after the war began, Joan was evacuated with her office in Customs and Excise from London to Blackpool. Later in the war Joan found herself in the women's branch of the army, the Auxiliary Territorial Service, and trained as a cypher operator. She was in France when Francis returned to England after four and a half years in the Middle East. They married and Joan returned to her duties at General Eisenhower's headquarters in France and then to Germany until she went back to England to have her first baby.

After Francis's release from the army they established themselves in a village in the foothills of the Scottish Highlands while Francis studied at Aberdeen University. They also kept bees for commercial honey production and produced more children, coping with the wanderlust, insatiable curiosity and inventiveness of the eldest and the inability of the youngest to digest substitute feed. This story ends with the family departing for Tanganyika where they spent the next thirteen very interesting years.

During the war Joan and Francis wrote many letters to each other. But there was one from Joan which was of such significance to Francis that he has it still. These are the circumstances under which it was written.

By May 1940 the Surrey Yeomanry battery, which had stayed in England, was considered fully trained and, with its companion battery of Sussex Yeomanry, was being issued with its equipment as a field regiment of Royal Artillery.

At the end of that month, the evacuation of the British Expeditionary Force from Dunkirk was under way and the Surrey and Sussex Yeomanry made room for some of the returning troops in their quarters at Dursley in Gloucestershire. The Regiment was under orders to be ready to move to France by the 15th June and it drew the remainder of its complement of 25-pounder guns direct from the factory on the 1st June.

After calibrating the guns at Okehampton, the first batch of officers and men left for 48 hours embarkation leave on the 10th of June. Joan was up north at Blackpool and there was no hope of Francis being able to get there and back in time so she came down by train to Dursley for a couple of days. On the morning that Joan wrote the letter which is appended to this preface, she expected that the Regiment would be starting on its way to France and she had to return to her work at Blackpool.

But on that day, the 14th of June, Paris fell to the Germans. On the 16th, the planned move of the Regiment to Southampton was cancelled and no British force was sent to France.

Joan and Francis next met for a few hours one evening at Aintree at the end of September 1940 before the Regiment sailed from Liverpool, and then not again until the end of March 1945 when he returned from the Middle East. They wrote to each other as often as they could but during all that time Francis kept this letter in his wallet with her photograph. It was a great source of consolation during those lonely four and a half years.

DURSLEY
14.6.1940

Francis, my own most dearest one,

The church bell has just struck five, but I've been awake for hours, counting the guns as they banged and clattered their way past my window, straining my ears for the Humber engine note, because you might - just might, go past. Though I know you're probably fast asleep in your narrow little bed.

I heard the guard come down from the gun park ages ago. I suppose Candy was there. Give him my best wishes, won't you?

I feel so forlorn now, I'm glad I'm going away.

Oh Fran, my own. I love you so. I wasn't very brave last night, I'm afraid, and yet I had made up my mind to be. 'You must smile as you wave me goodbye' - easily said, but not so easily done. My heart was torn from me when you went through that door last night. My place is with you, wherever you go - and oh my beloved, I need you so. You're so steady and dependable, so wise - I'm a very poor thing without you. See what a state I worked myself into before I came down here.

We'll have so many memories, won't we, to carry us on till next time - the tranquillity of the country, our walks, quaint inns, and Spartan lunches eaten, and stinging cider drunk. Such heavenly happiness, such bitter longing, such aching loneliness. It really has only strengthened our love.

I remember, darling, before the war, when you were dressed in blue. It made your eyes and your hair - not cropped then - so brilliant by contrast, that I thought you were quite the most wonderful man in the world. Now you wear khaki, and it scrubs my face, and you wear great heavy ugly boots, and they've cropped your bright curls, and yet, you're far more beautiful to me.

This isn't meant to be a letter, dearest. It's just a collection of thoughts, as they flash through my mind.

Did you cry a little, last night? Did you? I hope you did. Tears are no disgrace. Though I'm not worthy that you should cry for me.

It was like old times, praying together, wasn't it? I can still see us kneeling together, while shafts of golden sunlight mingled with the incense before the altar, and the singing was so sweet.

Don't forget things like that, my own. They are the fabric on which the story of our love is embroidered.

There's little I can say, dearest. My heart's too full for words of love.

Just, may God, who has been so very good to us, bless and keep you safe, that in His own good time, when the war is over, you may return to me in peace and happiness and safety.

It's nearly a quarter to six. You're washing and dressing only a little way from me. Do you feel me pulling you?

Bye bye, my sweet. You know my prayers will be offered up for you and for us every day. What more can I do?

Your own ever loving,

Joan

And such has been the fabric on which the story of our love was embroidered during the eleven years of this story and has been for these past fifty-seven years.

F.G.S.
Nedlands
14th February 1996

CHAPTER 1

UPHEAVAL

I met Francis in the February of 1939. It was the time when the civil war was raging in Spain and ripping the country apart. Some local organisation had rescued children of the beleaguered city of San Sebastian who had lost their parents in the fighting and had brought them to England, where they could be safe and properly fed.

The children were housed in the Oaks, an empty eighteenth century mansion close to my home. But that was only the start: they needed doctors, clothes, food, people to look after them, people who could speak Spanish. And all that took money. The rescuers turned to the local people. So on the cold Sunday morning of 14th of February, I found myself, most unwillingly, sitting waiting in someone's house for more people to arrive, and then we would all set out to do a house-to-house collection for the San Sebastian orphans.

I sat at a table, flicking through a magazine and wishing I were anywhere but here, having to knock on doors and beg for money. The door opened and my hostess came in, "This is Francis" she said, and left. I looked up. The newcomer was tall, slim and he had a mop of the reddest curly hair I had ever seen. Not ginger red, but a deep, rich copper, and a moustache to match. He smiled, and I found myself smiling back. "Do sit down", I said, "Would you like a magazine?" Then we talked, and it was slightly irritating to be interrupted and given our collecting tins and started on our way.

Somehow we managed to do our collecting together, and we did quite well; people were surprisingly kind. The worst part of it was that at practically every house, when the door opened, the rich, mouth-watering aroma of roasting Sunday lunch poured out on us: collecting for the orphans was a hungry job.

Time up, we handed in our tins and were told we'd done very well and that next Sunday the collection was on again. But I think that by next Sunday both Francis and I had discovered more important things to do than knocking on doors and begging for the orphans.

A few days later we met again by chance in the street near my home, and soon we became such close friends that we were like two halves of a whole. We were both busy, he with his banking exams and I with my language classes, but whenever we were both free we spent our evenings walking. In the hills behind Carshalton Beeches where I lived, you could walk for miles through beech woods and along empty lanes and we thought nothing of covering ten miles in an evening. My parents, who liked him, made no objection, so long as I was back by ten o'clock, which was my deadline.

Winter turned into a beautiful spring, and still we spent our evenings walking and talking - there never seemed quite enough time to say all we had to say.

Our world was wonderful, except for one thing: growing from a shadow to a menace, was the threat of war with Germany. It was difficult to understand how anybody could want a war: we didn't; nobody I knew did.

But the days passed and the threat did not go away: it grew bigger and blacker. One evening we sat on a stile and had a long talk about the political situation and the next week Francis joined the Surrey Yeomanry, our local Territorial artillery regiment. It had lost its horses after the Great War and had become a fully mechanised regiment of field artillery with 4.5-inch howitzers. He joined as a gunner and once a week he changed into uniform and went to the drill hall to train. It added nothing to his almost non-existent finances, but he did feel he was making his own small contribution to defence.

In August he and a few hundred other Territorials went to Larkhill for two weeks' training on the artillery ranges. I saw him off at Waterloo Station and it struck me, looking at that sea of khaki, that this is how the station must have looked during the Great War, before I was born.

Francis and his friends just managed to get their two weeks' training in before events overtook them. They left on 13th August and returned on 26th, a Saturday, and the next day we did one of our all-day walks, this time in Kent, from Westerham to Ide Hill, where we had lunch, and then back to Brasted.

The following Thursday at their weekly drill the Surrey Yeomanry were warned that they would be called up the next day, 1st September. It was on that day that we became formally engaged and two days later he gave me a ring with a small diamond, bought with his equipment allowance.

On the Friday, knowing that he was to be called up, he went to the bank in uniform, much to the disgust of Mr Woods, the Manager, who maintained to the last minute that there would be no war.

That was the day that Hitler's troops, in defiance of Mr Woods, invaded Poland. At three o'clock in the afternoon, over the radio, all members of the Territorial Field Army were told to report to their regimental depots.

Francis reported to his regiment, but that evening he came back to my house and spent the night there, returning to the drill hall the next morning, and the same thing happened the next day.

On Sunday, 3rd September, my father and mother and I listened to the wireless, and at eleven o'clock that morning, we heard the Prime Minister, Mr Chamberlain, announcing sadly and heavily that we were now in a state of war with Germany. As he ended, the first air raid siren of the war sounded. There were to be so many more. That time nothing happened.

That evening Francis again came home for the night and told us that his unit would be on the move the next day. During the evening the sirens sounded and again nothing happened. He left the next morning, early.

When he had gone, I went across the road to my friend and neighbour, Eileen, feeling in need of a little company of my own age. While I was there her father, who was Export Manager for the United Baltic Corporation, received a phone call from Mr Hazell, the UBC's agent in Gdynia, the Polish port. He had been very kind to Eileen and me when we had visited Gdynia in one of the UBC ships. Now he was ringing his chief to say goodbye: he had just succeeded in getting his wife and child out of Poland and over to neutral Sweden, and now he was off to join the Polish army. Over the phone we could hear bombs exploding in Gdynia.

"Can you get Warsaw on your wireless?" he asked, "Listen to it: you'll be able to tell how things are going. Goodbye."

We never heard of him again. We tuned to the Warsaw frequency: no programme; nothing but Chopin's tragic Revolutionary Prelude, over and over again, until, at last, it stopped and the station was silent. The Germans had arrived.

*   *   *

The Surrey Yeomanry was now split into two, the trained officers and men going down to Worthing where they joined the trained part of the Sussex Yeomanry, while the untrained, or only partly trained parts of both regiments joined together in Hove where they occupied the Cricket Ground. It was convenient for me: I managed to slip down by train for the odd evening, and even once managed a weekend. It was the period of the 'phoney war'; nothing much happened, so far as Britain was concerned, except that the RAF dropped a lot of leaflets on Germany, telling the Germans how much better it would be for them to stop fighting before we got really angry. It didn't seem to be one hundred per cent effective.

We who were very young and involved, were excited and stimulated by it all. It must have been rather like the first weeks of the Great War, with the boys we'd always known suddenly turning up looking very dashing in uniform. There was a complete blackout; no lights showed in any house, dark curtains, hurriedly run up, covered all windows and doors; there were no more lighted shop windows, no electric signs, no street lamps. Car headlights were so shrouded as to be practically useless; to find our way about and to avoid walking into things - a real danger - we used torches and even that had to be done cautiously: the slightest glimmer of light raised the cry, "Lights! Get that light out!"

Nobody knew what the next day would bring, and we lived life at a tremendously high emotional level. The country had been told to expect Hitler to send devastating air attacks against us immediately, and hearing about what he was doing in Poland we had no reason to doubt it.

London began to take on a strange and not very welcome face; gangs of men were digging slit trenches in all the parks and filling sandbags. Statues and monuments began to disappear behind ramparts of sandbags; entrances to big buildings began to dwindle in size as buttresses of sandbags were built up against them.

Torches became a necessity of life - you never went out without one. And moonlight suddenly became important as an aid to getting about after dark; for how many years had it been relegated to the crooners' vocabulary of moon, spoon and June? Later on that same moonlight became a mixed blessing indeed, when the dark of the moon was the time of peaceful nights and bright moonlight exposed targets to enemy bombers.

It was at the beginning of September that the children of inner London were evacuated with their schools to the

country and London became a city without children. It
was a heart-break. Rows of empty trains in the stations,
crowds of mothers with children, who were all carrying
their gas-masks in square cardboard boxes on strings
round their necks and each child had a large label pinned
securely to his front, with his name and address and
school on it. Some children were excited: it was rather
like a school outing for them. Others were in tears,
reaching arms back to their mothers as they were loaded
into the carriages. Some were beyond tears, silently
watching the organised chaos with big, scared eyes. And
the mothers, determinedly smiling, until the last door was
closed and the trains pulled out. Then the fixed smiles
slipped and they turned away in tears.

*   *   *

In October the Customs and Excise was transferred to
Blackpool and I had to follow my job. It was not so much a
transfer as an evacuation: most big Government
departments were leaving London in case there should be
aerial attacks which would stop them functioning. I was
very reluctant to go, for I should be too far from both
Francis and my parents to be able to see them very often,
but there were no two ways about it and I went. I and a
number of other girls of my age were billeted in guest
houses, and I suppose the men were billeted elsewhere. I
didn't realise then, how hard it was for them to be parted
from their families at the very time when they would most
wish to be with them, nor did I even wonder how they
would all face the extra heavy expenses they would have to
incur. I was too involved with my own troubles. I disliked
having to live in such close contact with a lot of people I
didn't know very well, and I was very homesick.
    The Branches in which we worked re-assembled in the
Imperial Hotel, on the front. It was an ornate, solid
Edwardian building which can't have changed much since
it was built. My own section found itself occupying the

Palm Lounge, all marble floor and grandiose fittings. Work resumed and bit by bit we made some form of social life for ourselves. A choral society was formed and a number of men and women began practising to produce the Gondoliers. I spent a lot of time writing letters. In the south, Francis was hard at work, training. As for my parents, my father had joined the Local Defence Volunteers, the forerunner of the Home Guard. There were no weapons to be had, but they were armed with pick helves and they wore yellow arm-bands with LDV on them.

Winter in Blackpool was not what I was prepared for. I had imagined that on the West Coast, with the Gulf Stream, it would be warm and comfortable in winter: not so. Blackpool is on an open unprotected coast, and during that winter there were terrible storms. What it must have been like for convoys battling through them I can't imagine, but at Blackpool the gales were so severe that on the front the winds picked people up, threw them down and blew them along, rolling them over and over like bundles of rags. Soldiers and airmen from nearby camps were stationed along the streets to help people cross over.

Christmas arrived and went, not much of a Christmas, away from home. Francis was in hospital with German measles. Just about everybody who could catch it did so, down in the south. He must have had it quite badly, for he was given sick leave and came up to me in Blackpool. My plump, motherly landlady took him in and made a fuss of him and he improved every day. Towards the end of his sick leave we managed a day or two walking in the hills round Garstang and that, I think, completed his convalescence. I saw him off at the station and that was that for some months.

In June the retreat from Dunkirk took place: his regiment had been preparing to go over to France and was stopped at the last minute after the fall of Paris. A few days later soldiers rescued from the beaches of Dunkirk fell into the beds the Yeomanry vacated for them and slept the clock round.   Francis said that when the first survivors arrived they looked like old men. The next day, when they were rested, washed and shaved, he realised that they were all about his own age. The later arrivals, who had formed the rearguard, were in much better shape and brought with them all their arms and movable equipment.

I think every church in England must have been packed at the time of Dunkirk; it seemed as if the people of England brought the troops home by sheer force of prayer. The men were crammed on a shelterless beach, between the sea and the enemy, and the ships could not get near enough to take them off. It was then that the fleet of small boats and yachts went across the tricky waters of the Channel and took men off the shore and delivered them to the ships, under constant air attack.   An incredible number of men were brought back. It was a miracle that the sea stayed calm enough for such tiny boats to make the risky crossing.

Britain lost a large part of her army in France, taken prisoner.   France fell; Norway, Belgium and the Netherlands had already fallen, and the whole weight of the German air attack was turned on the RAF in England as a prelude to invasion. When that failed it was followed by heavy air attacks on London and other big cities, specially in the south-east part of England.

I was at home on leave for some of these raids, and I shall never forget them. My first one began on a lovely, warm, sunny morning. The siren went, a nasty wailing noise that tied my tummy into knots. My father was at Custom House, at work, so my mother and I were alone. At the first wail of the siren, she picked up a loaded basket, put it on the kitchen table, said, "You'll want your bag, ration book, money, jewellery and something to do. Have you got a book?"

I ran upstairs and fetched my things. As I came down I heard some far-away thumps; "What was that?" "Anti-aircraft guns near the coast."

The thumps grew louder as guns closer to us took over the targets, and as the sound of the guns grew louder, it was mixed with the throb of enemy aircraft. The sounds soon became uncomfortably loud and Mother said, "Time to go to the shelter." We crossed the lawn and went down the steps of the shelter. It was dug deep into the chalk under the lawn, near the house. It was a small room, perhaps seven feet square, and had just room for two bunk beds with sleeping bags and pillows along one wall, a card table, two comfy chairs, an oil lamp, and a radio. Another small table held a primus and tea-making things and a small store of canned food. The floor was carpeted and the room looked very snug. To reach it you went down a steep flight of concrete steps, came face to face with a blank wall, turned sharp left, and there was the blast-proof door - well, we hoped it was blast-proof. It was made of rough and very heavy timbers and closed with the usual lock and also with two strong bolts, one at the top and the other at the bottom. It really was quite a comfortable room, which was just as well, considering how much time they had to spend in it.

Now to the noise of exploding anti-aircraft shells was added the whistles and crashes of bombs and the sharp crack of near-by guns. By this time we had retreated into the shelter and bolted the door. I felt very scared as each bomb fell a little closer, but then there was a pause and the next seemed to have passed us by. Quite suddenly, the guns stopped firing, and Mother said; "The Spitfires from Biggin Hill are going up."

We opened the shelter door and went up the steps. It was worth the risk from falling debris to watch them, tiny silver toys, wheeling and flashing almost out of sight, and then swooping down on the formations of bombers. But the bombers had brought their own fighter escorts and soon there were dog fights going on all over the sky which was scribbled with vapour trails. Now and again a bomber broke formation, released all its bombs to lighten its load, and turned for home with black smoke streaming behind it. There was the dreadful sound of a plane falling out of the sky, faster and faster, till the end came with a boom, and a pall of black smoke and parachutes drifted slowly down to earth.

The bombers and attacking Spitfires passed over. We became aware of quiet and in the quiet birds were singing. There was the odd clunk as pieces of shrapnel or bits of debris fell on the house, slithered down to the gutters and thumped to the ground. Down in the village, we could hear distant bells - fire engines or ambulances. And at last, far away a single high note, the All Clear.

*　　*　　*

In September, back in Blackpool, I had a very guarded message from Francis asking me to meet him in Aintree for an hour or two. I found an atlas and discovered that Aintree is south of Blackpool and north of Liverpool. I dropped everything - my boss was more than understanding - and caught a train south. The journey was difficult, to say the least. I had never been in that part of the country before, and as all the name boards had been removed from the stations to make things harder for the enemy - supposedly spies had no maps of their own - I was completely lost. It was a funny little train with basketwork seats and few passengers. When I asked of the carriage at large how many stops there were before Aintree, which would, of course, have no name board, from the grim looks and the sticky silence I realised they had cast me in the role of spy. I was near to tears when, as the train stopped at a station, a man stood up to get out, and, as he passed me, murmured out of the side of his mouth, "Next stop but one." And, at the next stop but one, to my relief, Francis was on the platform to meet me.

We had perhaps two hours together before I had to catch the last train back to Blackpool. It wasn't a very satisfactory two hours because, as we walked out of the station in the dusk, the air raid siren wailed and we had to cast around for shelter. Stations were not the best choice as railways were so often the target. The only place in view was a pub and, as we ran, the first planes were overhead. We reached it, opened the door, fought our way through the enveloping folds of the blackout curtain and found ourselves in a packed and rowdy bar.

The noise was terrific. We couldn't talk; in fact, in that uproar, I doubt if even a bomb could have been heard. We sat close together on a crowded bench, hand in hand, and the minutes ticked slowly by, and I tried to store up memories to keep against whatever was to come. This was no time for talking - even if we had been able to: in our silent communication it was a time of bonding, the bonding of our spirits that was to bridge all time and space.

And then it was time to go: the All Clear had sounded half an hour before; in the din I barely heard it. We left the bar and made for the station. It was dark by now. The little train with its odd seats was standing waiting. Francis gave me one last crushing hug, I climbed up into the train, it jerked and began to move. I leaned out and for a few moments saw his khaki figure, alone on the empty platform, motionless, one arm raised in farewell, and then he was gone.

He was twenty then. The next time we met he was twenty five.

The train was nearly empty. I sat in the dark carriage, too lost in grief for tears, and the train took me back.

Blackpool was cold, and the wind was blowing from the north, rain slanting along the streets and bouncing up from the pavements. The trams had stopped running for the night, and not a taxi was in sight. I set off, head down, collar turned up, and walked the mile back to my billet. The house was quiet and dark, everyone in bed - it was past midnight.

Up in my attic bedroom, I dropped my wet clothes on the floor and climbed into bed, chilled to the bone. But there was to be no relief for my misery in sleep: the hours crawled by as I lay, face to the wall, both hands pressed against it.

Daylight came at last. I got up, dressed and took my wet clothes down to the kitchen to be dried. My warm, kindly landladies exclaimed over my wet clothes, exclaimed over me; they were all sympathy and I was grateful, but I couldn't let them in: I was encapsulated in grief, no way out, no way in, and I stayed that way for a week. Then gradually, the numbness wore thin and left me, but the feeling that nothing mattered, nothing was worth while, stayed much longer.

It was really my elderly Aunt Gertrude living a few miles away, who pulled me out of it. She was a fund of common sense: after a sharp glance at me, she said,

"Well, he's on his way and grieving won't bring him back. You'd better do something for him, something useful. Have you started thinking about his Christmas parcel? You've not much time, you know."

*   *   *

Francis sailed from Liverpool on 1st October, 1940. The regiment was kitted out for the tropics and we supposed that he would be heading for Africa, though, with war-time security and the fear of spies, he might just as well finish up in Iceland as did the Kent Yeomanry.

As it turned out, the regiment did go to Africa, though it was a long time before I had any word at all from him.

The next four and a half years of his life are his story, not mine, and this is my story.

* * *

I began to get together a Christmas parcel for him. It wasn't the easiest thing in the world to do: there were so many silly little shortages; things that you took for granted, like pipe cleaners. For these things you had to keep an eagle eye on the shops that sold them and if you saw even a suspicion of a queue, to join it. We were all very good and law-abiding about this queuing business, no pushing or shoving and positively no queue jumping. That would have raised such a commotion that your face wouldn't have stopped blushing for months.

I collected small things he might like; tobacco, cigarettes - they were not a dirty word then - a cherrywood pipe, pipe cleaners, books. One of the girls with whom I shared my billet was engaged to a midshipman who didn't smoke; he generously donated some perique, Navy tobacco bound into a spindle shape with twine and dunked in - molasses, I think. It certainly smelled good.

Francis's parcel became the focus of a lot of interest among my friends and several of them made small contributions, such as paperback books. Aunt Gertrude, who was a wonderful traditional cook, produced a big parkin. This is a slab cake made of oatmeal, treacle, ginger and butter or lard. The best thing about it, apart from its wonderful taste, is that it should be kept for some time before eating, an impossibility in ordinary circumstances. But if it is kept, it gradually improves and mellows, or, as Aunt Gertrude said, it 'comes together'. We put it in a tin, sealed it with sticky tape and put it into a box with the rest of the small gifts, including a rather lumpy pair of khaki socks I had constructed (I had a feeling he'd do better to stick to the army issue, but it's the thought that counts) and a beautifully knitted scarf that was my mother's contribution. I wrapped it, tied it with string and then sewed the whole thing up in calico, provided by Aunt Gertrude. She had memories of sending parcels to her young brother Ned who was in the Camel Corps in the Great War. She said that was the best way to do it. I took it down to the post office during the Christmas rush and said a fervent prayer that it would escape the notice of the U-boats that were active in the Atlantic.

It was the end of March by the time my Christmas parcel arrived, and Francis's unit was in action at Keren in Eritrea, East Africa. He himself was in hospital in the Sudan, suffering from multiple small wounds to his back and arms, caused by fragments of rock, shrapnel and thorns. He had had a bad time in a forward observation post on the bare rocky mountains. He was in hospital for six weeks and when at last he returned to his unit, was told that there was a parcel waiting for him in a hollow baobab tree behind the gun position. He was delighted with it, specially with Aunt Gertrude's parkin which had 'come together' and was in first class condition. While he was in hospital his twenty first birthday had come and gone, uncelebrated; the parkin became his birthday cake and, shared out among his friends, it didn't last long.

*   *   *

1941 came. We hoped it would be a bit better than 1940. In Blackpool, few bombers reached our secure nest. Occasionally, during the night, sirens sounded, and I heard an enemy plane overhead: that odd engine note, "Mm, mm, mm", was unmistakable, but no bombs were dropped and we remained in strained and uneasy peace. Further south, it was very different. All the big cities were attacked; wave after wave of bombers dropped tons of explosives on them: countless houses were destroyed, thousands of people were killed, more were injured: Blackpool remained untouched.

I was tired of my job. It went on, month after month, just the same, while the war, so remote from us in

Blackpool, was gaining in intensity. I was bored, restless. I tried to join the WRNS, the Women's Royal Naval Service. I sent off my application and waited impatiently for an answer. It came. I was in a reserved occupation and could not volunteer. Conscription now applied to women as well as men and I must wait until I was called up and then I would have to go into the ATS, not the WRNS.

I joined the Civil Defence organisation as a part time telephonist and spent evenings and nights at the Blackpool nerve centre, taking part in practice operations. Practice, practice, never the real thing. I began to think about another parcel for Francis, to try and get it there in time for next Christmas. I knitted more socks, rather less bumpy than the first lot. That was all right, there was still plenty of wool to be had. But for other things, the shops were remarkably empty of suitable bits and pieces. Casting around, I saw, in the window of a hardware shop a very small Primus stove. It was a folding one, and what didn't fold took to bits and it all packed away into a small, flat metal box. It was Swedish, and the only one in the shop. The owner told me gloomily that there wouldn't be any more like that until after the war. I have never seen one like it since. I carried it home in triumph and packed it with more pipe tobacco and a book or two and the socks in the same way as I had packed the first parcel, boxed and paper-wrapped and sewn into a calico cover. I posted it and that was the end of the matter for me.

Months later I heard from Francis that it arrived by the first post to reach the regiment after they arrived in Tobruk. At the close of the East African campaign the regiment left Eritrea and went north into Egypt. Here they were ordered to discard everything but their essential army kit, and when that was done, they embarked in two Australian destroyers, *Napier* and *Nizam*, and sailed for Tobruk, to relieve the Australian artillery regiment which

had been besieged by the Afrika Korps for some time. All
the small comforts Francis and his friends had gathered
together during their months in Africa, were left behind
and never recovered, so the arrival of the little folding
Primus could not have been better timed.

Surrey Yeomanry

Royal Artillery

CHAPTER 2

OFF TO WAR

In October 1942, my long-expected call-up papers arrived. On the 9th, I packed up all my possessions and sent them home and, with a small case with my toilet things and writing case, a small pillow and two pillow cases, I caught the prescribed train from Blackpool to Lancaster to join the Auxiliary Territorial Service, the ATS. The train was packed with girls of my own age. In my carriage every seat was taken and it was full of ten highly individualistic young women, all dressed differently, all with different hair styles, some of them with masses of curls down to their shoulders, and all of them reacting in their own peculiar way to our unfamiliar situation. I couldn't imagine them being reduced, outwardly, at any rate, to a common denominator in khaki. I tried, and then gave up the effort. There was little talking as the train made its way north. I think we were too busy wondering what lay ahead, and not too happily at that. The girl sitting next to me and I talked now and then; she was rather nice. The train rattled and swayed on its way.

I was half asleep when the jerking of the train as it stopped at a station brought me back to full awareness. No signboard, of course, but a porter came along the platform, shouting, "Lancaster - Lancaster", and we gathered up our bags and trooped out. On the platform I now saw a number of girls wearing khaki tunics and skirts, khaki shirts and ties, caps and stockings, all very crisply turned out. Behind them a line of army trucks was drawn up, each with its tailboard down and inside I could see a bench along each side. I wondered vaguely what they were waiting for.

I didn't have to wonder for long. The army girls, all wearing NCO's stripes, set about us like a pack of

17

experienced terriers. We were sorted alphabetically, ticked off lists as though we were groceries, counted and ushered towards the line of waiting trucks and invited to climb in and sit down. I felt my last pair of silk stockings ladder as I scrambled up, but at least I didn't have to be hoisted in bodily by a soldier as some were.

As the last girls scrambled up, the tailboards were slammed into place, the trucks started up and we moved off in a convoy, but we didn't go far. By the time I had looked around me and remembered that a Duke of Lancaster was my supposed ancestor, the trucks were turning in at the gates of a barracks, and very grim and prison-like they were. The trucks drew up near some buildings and we were decanted. They drove off, leaving us standing about, clutching our small possessions and feeling lost.

But not for long. The NCOs who had met us rounded us up and hurried us to what I supposed was the hospital where army nurses told us to strip, weighed us, measured us, inspected us in ways that left me shaken and outraged, then gave us cards and told us to dress. I received a white card: "Go over there - where's your bag - take it with you - no you can't go with that girl, can't you see she's got a pink card you've got a white - don't argue, do as you're told". I did as I was told and joined the group and saw that they were all holding white cards. It was only then that I noticed that we were all joining groups, each group with a different coloured card. One group had all pink cards, another blue, another green. I was still meditating on this odd business when a girl wearing the three stripes of a sergeant came up to my group and said briefly,

"Follow me, please."

She didn't wait to see if we were doing so, but set off and we streamed after her, humping our bags, to a long, draughty barrack room, empty except for a line of iron-framed bunks down each side of the room, each with an upper and a lower bunk and a wooden stand that looked as though it was meant for a rifle. Half way down the room was a huge fireplace, the sort that could swallow a yule log. Into this room we were trotted and allocated a bunk - no free choice even in this, no "Would you care for the upper or lower?" and then, with another "Follow me, please" we were hurried off again, this time through a labyrinth of passages, to arrive at what must be the Quartermaster's Store. A male sergeant measured us, more or less, for our uniforms and doled out a mountain of kit: skirts, khaki, two; tunics, khaki, two; lanyard, green and rust, tunics for, one; caps, one; badges, cap, one; greatcoats, khaki, one; shirts, khaki, three; collars, khaki, six; studs, collar, two - or was it four?; knickers, khaki, celanese, three; stockings, khaki, pairs, three; shoes, brown, pairs, two; towels, three - NOT khaki; and so on. And brushes! the army must run on brushes: - brushes hair, brushes tooth, brushes shoe, brushes button, and on and on.

Back we hurried with our loads, still shepherded by our sergeant along those cold stone passages, until we reached our barrack room, being invited on the way to please note the name of our room, that they were all named after battles famous in the Regiment's history and, whatever we did, not to stray. I forget now what the name of our room was, Inkerman or Talavera or Badajos or something like that.

Back in the barrack room, somebody had lit a fire in the great fireplace and the room looked rather more homely. Now our sergeant pointed out the steel cupboards along the walls, one for each bunk. Each had just two small shelves; and now, to my dismay, she showed us, not only how each piece of kit must be folded, but the exact place it must occupy in the cupboard. I have never been really tidy and I began to feel that army life was going to prove for me a great mistake.

It was now time for us to cast off our civilian trappings and get into the new gear. It was not easy: everything did up the wrong way, the men's way, with buttons where the buttonholes ought to be, and never in my life had I had to cope with a collar that needed a stud at the back and another at the front to keep it attached to the shirt. Dressing was going to take me ages, and I hoped the staff were going to be understanding about it. We fumbled our way into our uniforms and, at last, dressing was complete. The sergeant, the corporal and the lance-corporal in charge of the fifty or so of us allocated to that room, came along and inspected us.

They seemed unimpressed: practically every tie had to be untied and knotted again - not mine! I'd worn a tie at school. Belts to our tunics would be done up on the middle of the three sets of holes, not pulled tight to show off our waists. And, hair . . . The sergeant smiled sadly. Hair, she announced, was to be worn an inch above the collar - no, as a dismayed clamour arose, there was no way out. One inch above the collar! Either you roll it up over a band made out of the top you cut off your useless civilian stockings or the regimental barber will make a thorough job of cutting it for you, though she had to say he was more used to doing short back and sides for the men than fashionable hair cuts. We digested this in silence and I thanked my lucky stars that I'd had forewarning of this and I'd had my hair cut and permed only the week before. A lot of nail scissors were lent around and civvy stockings cut up, and the change in hair styles began. There, said the sergeant cheerfully, that didn't look at all bad.

All our civilian clothes must now be packed away and our bags, marked with our names and newly acquired numbers, went away into store. My number - we must learn them quickly and never forget them - was W/163147. Now, that number and our names must be printed on every single piece of kit we had - including all those brushes. More work: it took ages, but at last it was done.

Now each girl received her bedding, three grey blankets and two sheets and the staff showed us how to make our beds. We did as we were told - it was becoming a habit - and I was grateful to the girl who had been called up ahead of me, the one who had warned me about hair and had advised me to take a small pillow; that was really good advice. It was small and soft and filled with feathers, a cushion really, more than a pillow, but such a comfort. I kept it all the time I was in the army.

The beds made to the satisfaction of the sergeant, she announced that it was lunch time and that we would now go on our first parade, Mess Parade, and for that we must, for some obscure reason, wear our caps. These, at the moment, straight from Q Stores, looked rather like a khaki version of a chef's hat and nothing at all like the crisp, flat-topped caps worn by the staff. We squashed down the tops as best we could and put them on, mostly, as was the fashion in the world we had just left behind, tilted fetchingly over our right ears. A fresh outburst from the staff! What had we done wrong now? Caps will be worn dead straight on the head.

Deflated, we re-arranged ourselves and shuffled out of the barrack room to stand outside in three more or less straight lines. All this just to go and eat! We right-turned, though we were not unanimous about that, and marched off, half in step and half out, to the Mess Hall. And it was here that my mother's faintly malicious words came back to me. "Aha!" she said, when I rang her up to tell her that I'd had my call-up papers, "Now you'll see how the other half lives!"

In the Mess Hall there were rows and rows of tables, each seating eight people, and we were marched straight to them and filed in to sit down, no choice of where or with whom we sat. The tables were of bare, scrubbed pine and were set with small plates and cutlery and with three large plates piled high with thick slices of fresh bread. To my astonishment, as they filed along the table to sit down, some of the girls at my table snatched at the bread as they passed the plates, grabbing several slices and then sitting guarding them with both hands, so that, by the time we were all sitting in our places, all three plates were empty. It was the duty of the girl at the end of the table to fetch more if needed and she did this, and the rest of us passed the new plateful around.

Nothing was said, but three days later, when I had relaxed enough to notice things better, I saw that nobody snatched at bread anymore.

I also found out, from somebody more knowledgeable than I, what some of the coloured cards meant: white was for the clean and sanitary, like me; pink meant that the recruit had 'things' in her hair; green meant that she had scabies (what was that?) and in either of those cases she could not be let loose in the community until she was cured, as such things were very catching. What the other colours meant I never did find out.

That first meal was good, plain but hot and plentiful. Half way through, an officer appeared and went from table to table, saying "Any complaints?" and we had to stop eating, sit up straight with our hands in our laps and someone had to say, "No complaints, Ma'am." The officer was accompanied by a large and beefy sergeant with a big red sash over one shoulder, and just looking at her I was pretty sure the officer didn't get too many complaints.

After the meal we went outside and got into three lines again and were marched back to our barrack room - whatever was its name? - where our sergeant told us that now we had some free time, ". . . except that now I am going to show you what to do to those uniforms so that I can take you out on to the Parade Ground without being ashamed of you."

She taught us to flatten our caps into the correct, sharp-edged shape: we must arrange them properly and then stand them upside down all night on our damp face-cloths. Our skirts, four-gored, we must fold just right every night, with the two side panels folded inwards, and laid carefully under our mattresses. ". . . and now, your buttons: you're going to have to put in a lot of work on them to get them right."

She was right. Sitting on our bunks, we set to work with Silvo, toothbrush, button-stick and cloth, scrubbing and polishing away at them until they began to lose their orange colour and take on an almost silvery sheen. Going from girl to girl, watching our efforts, the sergeant doled out little presents of praise. "That's much better, keep it up." "Yes, you've got the right idea" - and so on.

Eventually, she called a halt, and then, the trials and troubles of the day washed away in icy cold water, we went to bed, quite early, too. There was a radio high on the wall above the fireplace and Vera Lynn sang us to sleep. I didn't even hear the bugler sounding "Lights Out".

But, before that happened, there was one more thing. Among the intake was a red-headed girl, the sort of red-head who is automatically called 'Ginger'. We were all busy preparing for bed when she caught the all-seeing eye of the sergeant from the NCO's nook at the far end of the room. She had taken off her skirt, she had removed her tunic and her shoes. Then she made a dive for her upper bunk and was just snuggling down when the sergeant reached her.

"Ginger, come out of there! You can't go to bed like that! Come on, now! No nonsense, out you get!"

Ginger whined, "I ain't done nuthin' wrong, sarge: what've I done?" "You're not going to bed with your clothes on. What are your pyjamas for? Take your clothes off and put them on!" Ginger produced her new blue and white striped pyjamas and began to put them on over her shirt, but the sergeant was too quick for her,

"No, you don't. Out of those clothes, Ginger. Come on, no messing about!"

Ginger's whines turned to wails:

"I'll get me deff, sarge, I will!" But that was no help. The sergeant stood over her while reluctantly she took off the rest of her clothes and put on the pyjamas.

"Right, Ginger, that's a good girl. Hop into bed. Goodnight."

"Goodnight, sarge."

That set the pattern for Ginger. She bore no grudge at all, in fact, she became very attached to the sergeant, as if she was grateful for being looked after and chivvied a bit. I've always imagined that she came from a big family, pretty badly off and used to hard knocks. She was probably very homesick for them. Every night afterwards, when 'Lights Out' had sounded and with the room lit only by the flickers of the dying fire, she began her litany.

"Goo'night, Sarge."

"Goodnight, Ginger."

"Goo'night, Corpril."

"Goodnight, Ginger."

"Goo'night, Lance-corpril."

"Goodnight, Ginger."

And so it went on, including anybody she felt particularly fond of at the moment. I felt quite proud when she included me. Poor loving Ginger. I never saw her again after we all dispersed at the end of our 'square-bashing' course. I wonder what happened to her. Whatever it was, I hope it was good.

Auxiliary Territorial Service

CHAPTER 3

IN THE ARMY NOW

The next weeks flew by. I found myself in a world I could not have imagined in my wildest dreams. I learned - and how I learned! I was no longer embarrassed or affronted by the Orderly Officer's visit at meal times. I found I could salute an officer without losing my own dignity. I learned how to wear my uniform to the satisfaction of those whom I must obey. My skirt, folded accurately and pressed under my mattress at night, was crisply creased as required. Nobody's cap was flatter than mine. My shoes - imagine having to polish the bit under your shoes between the sole and the heel! - were taking on a beautiful shine and my buttons, after several hours spent sitting on my bunk polishing them, had lost their orange hue and were almost silvery. My hair, getting longer as time passed, and rolled round the top cut off one of my useless civilian stockings, was neat and the regulation one inch above my creaseless collar. Sometimes, as I sat on my bunk, working away at my kit, I looked round the barrack room at the neat heads and well turned-out owners of them, and found myself wondering who were the ones who had arrived with all the elaborate, piled-up curls, and the one-eyed, peek-a-boo Veronica Lake hair styles. It was impossible even to guess.

We spent a lot of time on the Parade Ground. This was a vast and sacred area of tarmac encircled by the grim blocks of barrack rooms. We must never run across it out of respect for the memory of the many soldiers of the Regiment who had drilled there and had died in actions a hundred years before. On this holy ground we were taught our drill by the long-suffering and patient staff. We learned how to form threes, with a blank file if we didn't divide exactly into threes. We learned how to march, all

25

starting off on the same foot, to mark time, to about turn, to dress from the right, which meant all getting into a straight line, and lots of other interesting manoeuvres connected with getting a bunch of people from A to B with the least possible confusion. We did a great deal of this sort of thing.

The Parade Ground was, as I have said, vast, and those late autumn days in the north of Lancashire were cold, damp and very foggy. Sometimes it was difficult to see the various squads drilling on the ground, and the voices of the instructors came only faintly, like bird calls, out of the fog. Occasionally, the front ranks, marching smartly away from their instructor, failed to hear the order to about turn; the rear ranks, nearer to the voice, about turned and marched obediently back, while the rest marched further and further away into the fog, those now at the rear, suddenly aware of the absence of footsteps behind them, looking piteously over their shoulders for someone - anyone - to come and rescue them before they marched right away into another dimension.

Apart from drilling, there were fatigues, the army's housework, to be done every day, not very nice, but necessary. Floors must be swept and polished, lavatories and washrooms, called ablution blocks, to be cleaned. I was shattered one day to find myself on my knees with a bucket of bitterly cold water and a scrubbing brush and half an acre or so of floor awaiting my attention, the first time I'd ever had a scrubbing brush in my hand. But on the whole, I got off fairly lightly where chores were concerned, possibly owing to the kindness of the staff, possibly owing to my blatant inefficiency.

Hair continued to be a vexed problem. At that time, with half the girls in the country modelling their hair styles on their favourite film stars, their hair was pretty elaborately done, and if a girl hadn't much money, she was not keen to demolish her set with a good daily brushing through, and there, I believe, lay the cause of lots of little troubles, and the reason for the number of pink cards handed out to nearly fifty percent of the intake. How the staff coped with a new intake every three weeks I can't imagine, for each case had to be treated before anyone could go to bed, and in my intake there were two whole barrack rooms full of these cases. I lived in such dread of picking up some 'things'. Our hair was inspected daily in case we did, but I never did.

Quite apart from the hair aspect, the staff worked like beavers and by the end of our three weeks' course, they had turned that train-load of civilian female individualists into a bunch of smart, alert, well turned-out and well-groomed women. It was really a transformation.

As our drill improved our officers decided to take us for short marches outside the barracks, and we swung along the road in fine style, marching in threes. I revelled in this sort of exercise, for I still missed the long tramps that I used to do with Francis before the war broke out. Gradually the marches increased in length until, not long before our three weeks' square bashing ended, we set out on a genuine route march, with the Commanding Officer at our head and led by the Regimental Band, big drum, leopard skin and all. It was great fun, if not exactly a marathon. The CO invited us to move to the right in column of 'rowt' and away went the band and then away went we, arms swinging, heads held high. The band's playing was timed to the step of an ordinary infantry regiment, which made rather long steps for us, specially for the smaller girls, but it didn't matter. We marched along with verve and pretended not to notice mere civilians on the pavements who said things like "Just look at those girls: aren't they marvellous?" and elderly gentlemen who said, "Smart turnout! Fine girls, eh?" Odd soldiers were a trifle more ribald, but our CO appeared not to notice them and we did our best not to giggle.

It can't have been a very long route march, surely. The band couldn't have done a really long one with their instruments, even though they didn't play all the time, but we were footsore and a trifle weary as we approached the barracks. The CO fell out and, as we marched past her, she called, "Now, up with those heads! Swing those arms! We march into barracks as smartly as we marched out!" And so we did, or, at least, I thought so. Later, after being dismissed, we went back to our barrack rooms where we were told by our NCOs how good we were and how much better than the people in other barrack rooms who were not half so smart. They then inspected our poor sore feet. There was some mourning over blisters, but not much.

During the last week in Lancaster we went through the hands of the army 'trick cyclists', the occupational psychologists, who gave us all manner of tests to discover where our talents, if any, lay. After several days of tests they told me that I was exceptionally mechanically-minded and how would I like to muster as an army driver? I was not best pleased: army drivers were privates.

I wanted RANK. I wanted something impressive and, poor clot, I said I'd rather do Cypher. (Cypher personnel had stripes in the lower echelons and in the upper ones they were commissioned.) The trick cyclists said, with a sigh, very well, have it your own way and don't say we didn't warn you, or words to that effect.

A few days later I was told that I was to be posted to Number Three Intelligence School in London when the next course started and that until then I was to stay where I was and try to be helpful. So, while the others, Ginger included, left Lancaster and dispersed to their various training places all over the country, two or three of us remained, rattling about dismally in empty, chilly barrack rooms, with our exquisitely tidy cupboards, our beautifully cared-for uniforms and the eternal Vera Lynn, piped in high above the fireplace, singing remorselessly from Reveille to Lights Out about nightingales in Berkeley Square and white cliffs and lights going on again all over the world. There didn't seem much likelihood of that in the immediate future.

Our postings came through at last! The three of us, glad to be doing something constructive after a week or more feeling like survivors on a desert island, packed our clean, new kitbags - that was another art form to be learned - received our travel warrants and movement orders, and said goodbye to the staff and to Lancaster. Now it came to the point, we left a little reluctantly. We'd enough sense to realise that though Lancaster had seemed tough at first, it had really been just a nursery school to prepare us for the army proper. Now we were going to the real thing.

A truck took us to the station, we were shown what the Railway Transport Office looked like and left there, another lesson to be learned. We discovered that the RTO is a sort of nanny to travelling soldiers, who are assumed to be quite incapable of moving about the country on their own. The RTO examined our movement orders, directed us to the right train, and off we went to London, looking extremely martial with our kitbags, respirators, tin hats, mess kits and mugs. It was a relief that, with all that stuff hung around us, it was cold enough to wear our greatcoats; at least we didn't have to carry them, on top of everything else.

On the train we met two other girls from other training depots who were bound for the same place as us. None of us had the slightest idea of what we were going into, or what the work would be about. It was the general idea of cypher that interested us.

We also found that travelling in uniform was quite different from doing the same thing as a civilian. In uniform we belonged to a big family and we could talk to uniformed people we didn't know and think nothing of it. Journeys, in spite of the fact that trains were cold and dark, unbearably crowded and almost invariably late, were fun.

When we reached London it was wrapped in fog, a real, old-fashioned, nasty-smelling pea-souper. We lugged our respirators and kitbags out of the train, threaded our tin hats on to our arms and fastened them under our epaulettes and trudged through the gloom to change trains.

By the time we reached our destination, Herne Hill, our numbers had increased by the addition of several men and conversation was general. At Herne Hill, to the disembodied cry of "'Erne 'Ill! 'Erne 'Ill! This side out! This side out! 'Erne 'Ill!" - a useful bit of advice to stop you getting out the wrong side and falling on the live line or under another train - we got out with all our bits and pieces, found the RTO's office and were told how to find the School. Shouldering our loads we walked out of the station and into complete and utter opacity.

It was a job to find the School. The short winter day was drawing in and the fog thicker than ever. In a tight group we began to feel our way along the pavement, hands touching fences. The houses here were big old Victorian mansions, set far back from the road and concealed behind thick shrubberies. There were no numbers to be seen, even with a torch, and of course, there wasn't a gleam of light anywhere. Cold, tired and hungry we groped our way on, peering at decaying gateposts, hoping to find a number, and at last, when we were beginning to think we were really lost, we found it. In a tight group we turned into a driveway and began feeling our way up the gravel path through an overgrown shrubbery. Water splashed over us as we pushed our way through low-hanging branches; it was as black as the inside of a cow, as one voice elegantly put it. But after what seemed like an age without hope, and narrowly missing falling into the unfenced basement area, there were the steps and we climbed up to a blank front door. Could this possibly be the place? Not a sound came from inside, no voices, not a glimmer of light. The place looked as if it had stood empty for years. One of the men fumbled for the bell, one of those brass knobs that you hauled on, and seconds later there was an answering clang far, far away. We stood around, like a bunch of carol singers, waiting uneasily for something to happen. Time crawled by.

Footsteps approached the door and it creaked open just a slit, revealing nothing but blackness. Unseen eyes observed us, the door opened further and we were ushered quickly inside. Behind us the door creaked shut, bolts slammed home, the blackout curtain was pulled aside and we were in a bare, lighted hall.

The NCO who had opened the door collected our movement orders and led us out of the hall and I had my first sight of a requisitioned private house. The rooms were high-ceilinged and well proportioned and must have been beautifully furnished - large unfaded squares of colour on the wall showed where pictures had hung - but now emptied of all their previous character, they were filled with army tables and chairs, some like class rooms with blackboards and others more like the Mess Hall at Lancaster.

The course began next day. The work was not difficult, the most necessary thing being accuracy. And of course, security, which was drummed into us all round the clock. Remember your responsibilities to the fighting men! Careless talk costs lives! Remember the penalties for breaches of security! After a few days of this I began to feel that the entire responsibility for the conduct of the war had fallen on to my shoulders.

The course was an eyeopener: we were all back at school, our army teachers a little less patient with us than the staff at Lancaster. The work was fascinating; puzzles had always attracted me and now they were my full-time

job. And I never could have believed there were so many
ways of concealing a message.

At the end of the two-weeks' course I was posted back to
the north, to Bradford, as a qualified Low Grade Cypher
Operator with a brand-new single stripe. A Lance-
Corporal, no less! Rank at last!

Royal Corps of Signals

CHAPTER 4

BRADFORD

Winter is perhaps not the best time of the year to visit a northern industrial city and Bradford made no great effort to greet me. I was met at the station and driven to what must once have been a beautiful house, but, like the one I had just left, army occupation had hardly improved it. I never saw much of the house itself, apart from the room I was allocated for my work, but I shared it with the Intelligence Officer and, from my desk through full length windows I could look out on rolling lawns - not quite as smooth as velvet, as they probably had been before the war, but satisfying enough. Another girl on the course had been posted to the same place, so we were able to alternate our duties, and keep at least a day-time watch. We were the first cypher operators to be posted to this very small headquarters, and there was practically no provision for security, but within days, we found part of that delightful room had been partitioned off and bars fitted to the window, making a small cell within the room, with a door that we were to keep locked.

I found that several houses in a street close by had been requisitioned by the army and fitted up with army beds and the traditional 'biscuits'. These were square cushions - biscuits is a much better word for them - three to a bed. They weren't bad if you were lucky enough to be given three of the same thickness, otherwise they had their drawbacks.

I stayed in Bradford about a year; the work load was very light, too light, and little 'live' traffic came in. Mostly, it was practice messages and messages concerned purely with cypher, nothing world-shaking, nothing of historic importance, nothing, really, much better than the Customs work I had been doing before I was called up. I don't remember much about it now, which seems to be the way the mind often treats bad times. Looking back, it always seems to have been cold and raining. There must have been many beautiful, warm, sunny days in spring and summer, and not far away lay some Yorkshire moors and fells, but my sharpest memory is of streets of grey cobble stones, houses of grey, sooty stone, roofs of wet grey slate, and I was homesick, homesick for my family, for Francis and for the south.

One of the better memories is of the Signals Office, a big, light building set in the garden, close to the kitchen and our Mess. The NCO in charge was a sergeant, a big, fair, bluff man, a despot with the kindest heart imaginable. It was to this warm, companionable place that I fled when the isolation of my little cell pressed on me. Here he showed me the mysteries of the Fullerphone, which carried his morse messages along telephone wires to their destination in security. But, best of the lot was the pigeon loft, from which, every day, we sent out carrier pigeons. That was pure enchantment. He allowed me to take the bird from its cage and hold its strong body in my two hands while he rolled up the message, written on some-thing that looked like cigarette paper, fitted it into its tiny cylinder and clipped it to the bird's leg. Outside, he let me start the pigeon on its way, sweeping my hands upward and letting it go. Just as my hands opened I would feel the tremendous surge of its muscles as the wings beat strongly and it flew up and up, circled once or twice and disappeared behind the trees. That was a marvel that never failed to thrill.

Small islands of memory in a sea of forgetting: the kindness of a family who owned a grocery store and post office, who took me in, rather like a stray cat, gave me meals and hot baths and a warm cosy fireside to sit by. And it was in Bradford that I went to my first ever concert of classical music. There was a fine symphony orchestra there, and the people of Bradford appreciated good music. Goodness knows why classical music had never made an impact on me before: it was not for want of my mother's trying. She had taken me to several operas, as she had taken me to the Old Vic to see Shakespearian plays, and she had taken me to Sadler's Wells to see a number of ballets, but somehow this concert at Bradford was the first time the music had really impinged on me. That concert opened a door of escape for me from the distasteful aspects of army life.

The year ground on. I stuck it out - I had to. I did two short stints on detachment, one in Nottingham and one in York, and both times I was billeted in a workman's cottage. I have forgotten all about my time in York, except the beauty of the city: in other circumstances I could have spent weeks wandering around there, but I wasn't on leave. Of the work side the only thing that has stayed with me is my first seeing that well-known security poster, stuck up on the wall of the Cypher Office, "BE LIKE DAD: KEEP MUM" which struck me as being tremendously funny - it still does.

In Nottingham I was billeted with a man and his wife who lived in a row of houses opening straight on to the pavement. Behind the house was a small yard and beyond that, the family lavatory, one of a block of four, all joined together, serving our house and the one next door and two houses in the street behind us. The man of the house, Mr Charles, worked in the nearby tobacco factory; his wife had been in service in one of the big houses near Nottingham, where she was cook. Her cooking was a revelation. My Mama was a good, conscientious, plain cook: she approached cooking with a sort of "It is my duty and I will" attitude, but she didn't enjoy it - it was a chore, keeping her from much more interesting occupations. But Mrs Charles was an expert.

Her house was fiercely clean and polished, and it must have been a hard job to keep it that way in an industrial city. Every day she swept and sluiced down the pavement outside the front of the house, she scrubbed and whitened the front step and polished the outside window ledges - all this practically in the shadow of the factories which belched out sickly sweet fumes over everything. She showed me her parlour: carpet, uneasy chairs, unused piano with the top adorned with a plush runner with bobbles and a great array of family photographs, a table in the window with a statue of a small boy fishing, turned to face outside, to make a nice view for passers-by. While I was there we never used the parlour; we lived snugly in the kitchen, with two spavined armchairs, one each side of the range where the fire never went out and, when the fire door was opened, the flames made little dancing points of light on the polished shiny bits. There was a rag rug in front of it, all black and red and blue, and the kitchen table had a chenille cloth over it, dark red with more bobbles and the whole kitchen full of the smells of her wonderful cooking.

Mr and Mrs Charles lived well where food was concerned, far better than my parents. He worked at the factory, but he spent most of his spare time either working on his allotment or fishing in the river. He brought home his catch and she gave it her expert treatment. The allotment gave them more vegetables and fruit than they could use. She baked fantastic pies; while I was there they were stuffed with red currants and strawberries. The pastry was a feathery dream, tasting of butter, and this in war-time, with the ration two ounces a week per person.

The answer was, of course, the system of barter which grew up naturally among small producers of food. The Charleses had more vegetables and fruit and, sometimes, fish, than they needed; one neighbour kept bees and exchanged honey for fruit and vegetables. Some of his sugar allowance for winter feeding, combined with spare fruit, made jams and bottled more fruit in syrup. A man they knew who ran a few cows didn't need his ration of cream and butter, another kept a few hens which the Charleses helped to feed, and round and round went the small surpluses easing life for everybody and making it much more pleasant.

My stint in Nottingham over, I packed up my kit and said goodbye to the Charleses with real regret; they had been so kind to me, much more so than they had to be to a strange girl billeted on them for a few weeks. Back I went to our bare, empty house with the army beds and the three biscuits, back to my little cell in the Intelligence Office.

My time in Yorkshire came to the usual abrupt army end when one of the Signals girls came out of the Signals Hut carrying a teleprint posting me back to Herne Hill to do a High Grade Cypher Operator's course. Back to Herne Hill, only a short train ride from home. I repacked my kitbag, said goodbye to my off-sider, took respirator, tin hat, greatcoat, mess kit, mug and my precious little pillow, and looking like a slightly bandy Christmas tree, took the train for London.

This time I arrived in broad daylight, with not a wisp of fog. It was summer, and between lectures we took our mugs of coffee out into the garden and drank it in the shade of an old mulberry tree, the only one I'd ever seen. The fruits were ripe and falling, sweet, black and full of juice, tasting like wine.

On this course we were no longer a bunch of apprehensive recruits; we were experienced Low Grade Cypher Operators. But with us this time were quite a few officers, coming into Cypher for the first time, and some of them were Americans. The work was hard and complex, and I began to realise how very elementary my work had been up to now. There was so much to learn, to remember, to understand. Nothing could be written down, everything committed to memory. Any writing done in the lecture was collected for burning, and the three sheets next on the pad went too. Instruction went on all day, with brief pauses for coffee and a rather longer one for lunch, to give us time to get round to the Mess. I think everyone must have felt the strain - I know I did, and at the end of the day's work my neck was stiff and aching with tension. Only one thing cheered me on, the vision of the prize at the end: we would graduate at the end of the course as commissioned officers!   Rank at last!   No more Mess Parades! No more Kit Inspections! No more Pay Parades! Hooray! Life would be so much better in so many ways! If, of course, I passed. That was a point. My only worry was, how to break the news to Francis? A loner and a rebel to his boottips, he was still a Gunner, although a Specialist. How would he take it? I didn't want to upset him. Perhaps it would be better not to tell him; he could go on addressing his letters to L/Cpl Bardwell and I'd get them just the same. The name wasn't all that common.

When we were given free time, I took a train home, a round-about trip, but even an hour or two was well worth the effort. The bombing wasn't as bad now, in fact, our lectures were often interrupted by the ear-splitting racket of wave after wave of bombers flying overhead, formation after formation that stretched right across the sky. You couldn't begin to count the aircraft, and wonder of wonders they were OURS, not THEIRS, and all heading for Germany. I felt little pity for the Germans on the receiving end of such an onslaught: they'd made life hell for us and now they were getting it back. That was all. I felt no pity for them at all until I arrived in Frankfurt and saw what life had become for them - what it would have become for us if the war had swung the other way.

The course lasted four weeks, four long weeks. But at last the final week came. The entire course was pretty subdued, even the more light-hearted American officers;

we were all tired, strained and anxious about the results. To go back to Low Grade Cypher work after all we had learned would be too much. But would we be permitted to go back, with what we had learned? Contemplating some of my most shameful blunders, I decided that when I'd been told I'd failed and been flung out, I'd do as the trick cyclists at Lancaster had advised, and re-muster and train as an army driver. Then I couldn't, as the officer with the green tabs and the gold braid had said we might, send a whole division to their death by making a mistake, could I? Not if I was just driving a truck? I remembered that man's visit only too well. He was giving us a pep talk about the vital importance of our work, the need for complete security and utter accuracy. After he'd gone on in this way for some time, some fiend inside me made me say, very quietly,

"What about the human factor?"

He heard me! He must have had ears like a lynx. A tide of purple rose up above his khaki collar and he shouted,

"Stand up whoever said that!" Absolutely terrified, I stood up, my face rivalling his own.

"Say that again!" he invited me.

"How about the human factor?" I whispered. If possible, his face went a deeper purple, reminding me of the mulberries on the lawn outside.

"THERE IS NO SUCH THING as the human factor. Do you hear me? THERE WILL BE no such thing. GOT THAT?"

"Sir", I whispered and sank down as low as I could get in my seat. He could shout, but he wasn't right. I knew it in my bones.

The last day of the last week of the course came, the day of reckoning. We assembled. The CO read out the results, mercifully, just the passes and those in alphabetical order. I passed . . . .

When the murmurs of congratulation were over, he invited all officers present to leave the class room, which they did. Then, looking very ill at ease, he told us that he was the bearer of bad news: the War Office had decided to economise, an amusing exercise in war time, and in their wisdom, they had decided that the first step towards cutting the costs of the war should be to reduce the rank of new High Grade Operators (on whom, we had just been told, so much depended, who held, like the gilded Staff, the lives of thousands in their hands) from commissioned rank to the rank of Sergeant.

Having broken the news, he left the room quickly. There was absolute silence. Then somebody said a very rude word and apologised. There was another silence. Someone said, bitterly,

"The bastards! They charged my mother for the blanket they buried my father in!"

"Bloody hell," said another voice in conclusion, "what fools we were not to have expected it! Let's go down to the pub."

So we did.

CHAPTER 5

BACK TO THE NORTH

The course broke up a few days later and I don't think any of us was sorry to leave. There was time for me to make a short visit home, and I came back by bus, suddenly conscience-stricken when I noticed I hadn't changed out of my battle dress blouse and trousers before I left the camp. We were only supposed to wear that rig within the confines of the military area; presumably we might have hurt the delicate sensibilities of the civilian population if we had been seen dressed in the same way as the men, though I should have thought that the civilian population would have become hardened to much worse sights after these years of bombing. However, I was lucky and managed to get back into camp without meeting anybody who could put me on a charge. The next morning I left Number Three Intelligence School and caught a train to my new posting, Preston, in Lancashire. Having started my career in the north of England I didn't seem able to break away from it.

The train was packed with troops, as trains always were, and there wasn't a seat to be found, but I settled down comfortably in the corridor with dozens of other service people. My kitbag made a useful seat, and the Mess had provided me with a hefty pack of sandwiches for lunch.

At Preston railway station a Tilly was waiting for me, quite the smallest army truck I had ever seen; it looked very much as if it had been converted from an Austin Seven. I piled in with my baggage and we set off for my new formation, which turned out to be 4th Anti-Aircraft Group. The headquarters was set up in a large country house in extensive grounds a few miles outside Bamber Bridge. The offices were all in the house itself, as were the Officers' Mess and their quarters. The rest of the person-nel were accommodated in huts in the grounds.

The next day I received my new shoulder flashes, which were two squares of scarlet cotton with an arm shooting an arrow straight up into the air. These had to be sewn on to the sleeves of both my tunics as neatly as possible. For some reason this badge of AA Command caused us to be known as Cupid's Cavalry.

It was bitterly cold. I shared half a hut with two other Cypher Sergeants and we had the wonderful luxury of a tortoise stove in the hut. It was absolute heaven to come in after a shift to warmth and comfort, but only too often our tiny allowance of coal ran out much too early.

There was a great heap of coal in the camp, but somebody, probably the Quartermaster, had had it surrounded with wire. I became expert at crawling through that wire to reach the lumps which, as the icy weather continued, shrank further and further back from the wire. From the speed with which the gap increased I can't have been the only wire-crawler.

News of the shrinking coal heap must have filtered through to the Quartermaster, for he reacted by running more barbed wire round and then in true army fashion, he whitewashed the heap. Where we took coal from would now show up black.

For a while the heap remained snowy white and inviolate while the coal thieves thought out their next move. Then the weather changed: a gale straight out of the north brought a blizzard. I went on duty heavily wrapped up with khaki ankle socks over my stockings, gum boots, two pairs of khaki gloves and a thick khaki scarf (a present from my mother; khaki wool was coupon-free) over my cap and ears, tied under my chin and the ends tucked down my greatcoat. The tiny ration of coal lasted no time at all for girls who were working all round the clock. It was too much. Quite a few must have crept out that night, though I myself saw nobody at all. Snow lay thick on the heap for days, and when it finally melted away, there was the Q's precious heap, visibly smaller and with very little whitewash left.

A few months with 4th Ack-Ack set me thinking that I could do with a warmer climate and wondering whether I could possibly get nearer to Francis, who was now in or near Cairo. Cairo had a set-up that used people with my qualifications and it would be much more pleasant all round than up here, far away from him, and from home too. It was now Christmas 1943. I celebrated it by putting in my application for overseas service and, having done that, prepared to celebrate Christmas army style.

Christmas Day in the army is by tradition the day when sergeants wait on other ranks, but I'm very far from clear in my mind how it came about that female sergeants were detailed to take morning tea to the male sergeants. Perhaps the Regimental Sergeant-major had something to do with it. It was a surprising experience, but all in good clean fun and I had to go back to my hut and tidy up my hair before going on duty. I worked till midday, if you could call it work, for nothing came in except practice messages wishing everybody a happy Christmas. When I was relieved I went over to the Sergeants Mess for lunch, where we were waited on by Officers, who, having been entertained in the bar with the usual generous drinks by the Regimental Sergeant-major, were in fine fettle. That was the day when unwittingly I added a little something to the festivities and earned the Mess President's unending disapproval. The Colonel had decreed that the 'gals' as he called us, could take their turn behind the mess bar, and help the men on busy evenings. Christmas Day was the day for my initiation into working behind the bar. Never in my life had I even been near one, and I was mystified by all the different drinks. Moreover, the Mess Sergeant was too hurried to have time to explain elementary things to me, such as which was the whisky measure and which the sherry. So I happily doled out the precious Scotch with the largest measure I could find, and it wasn't till stock taking the following day when all concerned - except me: I was on duty - were feeling delicate, that my villainy was discovered. I believe the Colonel decided straight away that it was not worth the trouble having women doing bar duty and we were all excused further adventures in that line.

That year crawled by. Far from home, with letters from Francis few and far between, I felt depressed and lonely. I have never been an enthusiastic party-goer: just a few friends together, quietly talking over a meal or a drink, that was my idea of a good time. Rowdy parties over at the Mess when we entertained American soldiers from a nearby camp, who didn't want to 'dance', but to do a series of extraordinary contortions called jitterbugging, was for me, out.

The work too, which at first had seemed so exciting, so thrilling, I now realised was mostly routine, and quite a lot of it was just practice. We were quite a long walk from the small village where the bus stopped, and the village quite a long way from the nearest big town. We went in occasionally, and saw a film, but the walk back along unlit lanes squelchy with the passage of tanks, and in pouring rain, was unattractive.

Soon after Christmas I was due for leave, and found myself with a whole seven days and a railway warrant for home. I could hardly believe my luck. In the Cypher Office things were hotting up: everywhere there was talk of the Second Front. It couldn't be long now before the war really erupted. I packed my overnight bag, took shoulder bag, respirator and tin hat, squeezed myself and my kit into that tiny Tilly and was driven to Preston Station. It was dark by the time we arrived, and the queue at the

RTO's office long. By the time I was cleared with him it was nearly time for the London train to depart, and from the furthest platform. I ran up the steps and on to the great iron bridge over the line and joined the crowd running to catch the train, and I was nearly over when in the dark somebody barged into me, sending me reeling sideways against an iron stanchion. I slammed into it and the full impact went on my right hand, which was carrying my overnight case. I felt a jab of pain, but there was no time to stop and I ran on.

Whistles blew and the train jerked into motion as I made my way down the corridor hunting for a seat. The train was packed, and almost everybody was in uniform. I was losing hope of finding a seat and steeling myself to sit on my case all the way from Preston to London, when a soldier called out,

"In here, Sarge, there's just room for a little one."

What a relief! He put my case and greatcoat up on the rack for me and I sat down. It was only then that the pain in my hand made me look at it: the middle finger was sticking out at a most peculiar angle. Something was badly wrong.

"Oh, look." I said to the carriage at large. "I've hurt my finger."

They looked. One of them got up and went into the corridor. I heard him saying,

"Is there a doctor on the train?" He came back quickly:

"There's no doctor, but this chap's a Sick Bay Attendant." and ushered in a sailor who picked up my hand.

"Let's look at it , love." he said. "Well, you've dislocated it. How on earth did you do that?" I told him

"Well, now, I'll put it back. This is going to hurt, OK?"

"OK." I said, shutting my eyes. I felt him take the finger, and give a quick strong pull. There was a click, and when I opened my eyes, the finger was back in place. I began to thank him, but I couldn't see him properly. Things had got a bit misty and there was a roaring in my ears, then nothing.

I was in the corridor, lying flat. Somebody's greatcoat was over me, and someone was making my face wet with cold water. Somebody else was saying,

"Anybody got a flask?" and it seemed time to say something myself.

"I'm all right," I said, and with some help I got to my feet.

The rest of the journey was as pleasant as a trip can be in an unheated, almost unlit and very overcrowded train; my carriage seemed to be full of elder brothers, all concerned about me.

Not far outside London sirens were wailing and the train stopped, as they always did during a raid, so that no signal lights or sparks could betray our position. Bombs began to fall as the Luftwaffe felt for the railway lines, each one closer. The last was much too close for comfort and the rain rocked with the blast, but to my relief it must have been the last of the stick. A quarter of an hour later the All Clear sounded, and the train jerked and began to move.

It was broad daylight when we reached London. I said goodbye and thanks to my companions, and took the Underground to London Bridge Station. A train was standing on my platform. I put down my case, found my ticket and presented it to the ticket collector at the barrier.

"You've got a long wait, Sarge," he said, "That was a pig of a raid last night and things are upside down, no gas, no water and precious little power. Your train won't move for a good hour and a half. Do you want to go and find a cupper and something to eat?"

"Not really," I said, "What I really need is just to get some sleep."

"Tell you what," he looked round cautiously, "Tell you what: just you nip along and find yourself a carriage and kip down. You look tuckered out. I'm not supposed to, but I haven't seen you, see?"

I found myself a carriage: it wasn't difficult - the train was completely empty. I stowed my gear on the rack, noticing that my finger had now turned blue-black from the knuckle to the nail. I was glad that at least I had something to show for all the fuss. I lay down full length on a seat and closed my eyes. An hour and twenty five minutes later I was awaked by whistles and the train starting. Its motion rocked me off to sleep again, some inner alarm clock waking me up just three minutes before my station, and as we slowed to a stop I opened the door and hauled myself and my kit down on to the platform. Home again. For seven whole days.

*   *   *

The war ground on - 1944 now. There were sporadic raids on German installations on the French Channel coast, costly in lives, but lifting the spirits of the people in the occupied countries, who were badly in need of a glimmer of hope. It was fascinating to listen to the BBC broadcasts to the Resistance groups in France. The messages made no more sense to the uninitiated than the enciphered messages I dealt with daily: the names of the addressees were coded and the content of the messages obviously gave information on the dropping of agents and supplies. The stalemate in Europe seemed to have gone on forever, so that even such obscure messages brought reassurance that somewhere, somehow, things must be moving towards a second front; things of which even we were completely unaware. The Second Front, it was in everybody's thoughts.

Spring came late that year. We were all keyed up. The people with whom I worked, and people like us, were certain that something must happen soon. It did. British troops landed in the south of Italy and began to fight their way northwards. A landing at last, an attack on what Churchill called the 'soft underbelly of Europe'.

The longed-for, yet still amazing news, that we had made a landing on the Channel coast of France, broke in June. It was almost too much to believe. I had been on duty till midnight and was still asleep when another Cypher Sergeant came crashing into my hut with the news. I scrambled into my uniform and we ran over to the Mess where a crowd had gathered round the radio, hungry for the smallest scrap of information. There appeared to have been landings on the Normandy coast, at what they called Utah and Omaha Beachheads, where the American troops had come ashore, and to the east at Gold, Juno and Sword Beachheads, where the British troops had landed.

*   *   *

The Normandy landings and my posting to Supreme Headquarters occurred practically simultaneously. Somebody in the postings department of the War Office with a little time on his hands obviously had a sense of humour. She wants to go to Cairo does she? We'll give her overseas service! Let's post her to SHAEF.

SHAEF

CHAPTER 6

SECRET DESTINATION

I left 4th Ack-Ack two days after D-Day; after all the years of retreat and of those small raids on the French coast we could hardly believe that at last the army was back on French soil. And here I was, off to join the Supreme Headquarters Allied Expeditionary Force (SHAEF), where I'd be in the middle of the running of the offensive, at its very nerve centre. No more practice traffic for me. From now on it would be the real thing.

I packed my kit; a truck took me to the station and left me there. I found the RTO and presented my travel papers. To my surprise, instead of glancing at them and handing them back straight away, he looked hard at me and then slowly,

"Well, of course, I can't tell you **where** you are going - you'd better take the 10.15 train to London - you're in plenty of time - and report to the RTO when you get there."

And that was all he was inclined to say. I picked up my baggage and went to the door, feeling short-changed and slightly ruffled: it's nice to know where you're bound for, specially when everything you possess is distributed about your person or in the kitbag you're humping. At the door I looked back. The RTO had called a number and was deep in conversation in a very low voice. He caught my eye, stopped speaking and made an ushering gesture, "OK, Sergeant, that'll be all." I left, with the probably groundless feeling that he was talking to somebody about me.

The London train was, as usual, packed to the doors. Most of the passengers were Service personnel and they made room for me in the corridor. I sat on my baggage and ate my parcel of sandwiches in a big, cheerful crowd.

London was vast and noisy and full to bursting of troops of every nation you could think of, uniforms and caps of every shape and size. I found the RTO's office, joined the queue, waited my turn; it came at last. The RTO put down his steaming mug of coffee, looked at my movement order, asked for my pay book, checked it against the movement order, looked hard at me and, like an echo of his brother officer in Preston, said,

"Well, of course I can't tell you where you're **going.**"

And then he said that perhaps if I went to a certain house in Bryanston Square I might find someone to help me on my way.

My tummy was empty, my lunch-time sandwiches long forgotten, my new shoes hurt, I had a blister on my heel and the day was wearing on. Joining SHAEF had lost its glamour. Where was I going? How could I get there? How could I possibly get there if nobody was willing to tell me where it was? Where was I going to sleep? Where was I going to get something to fill this aching void inside me? And where, oh, where, was Bryanston Square?

Morale at an all-time low, I lugged kitbag, greatcoat, tin hat, respirator, new shoulder bag, blistered heel and myself, outside the station, wondering what to do next. I couldn't find it just by walking, and from the behaviour of the two gallant RTOs I'd better not wander about asking all and sundry where the wretched place was.

And then, right out of the blue, the miracle happened; well, it was a miracle in those days. A taxi came cruising slowly past and it had its little flag up - it was actually and unbelievably looking for a fare. I waved frantically, he saw me and pulled up. I scrambled in, narrowly escaping getting jammed in the door by my gear.

"Where to, ducks?"

"To Bryanston Square."

And off we went; it was as simple as that.   I disentangled myself from the kit slung round me, sat back and relaxed for the first time since reaching London.

It was quite a long ride - to this day I have no idea where we went, but then the taxi slowed and stopped. The cabbie put an arm back and opened the door.

" 'Ere you are, love, 'Ope somebody's 'ome."

It cost me half a week's pay, but it was worth every penny of it. I got out, dumped my kit on the pavement, and looked at the house we had stopped at. It was tall and dark, with no sign of life at all. It looked as if it had been empty for years. Behind me, the miracle taxi started up and moved off and I felt a brief flash of panic; suppose the house really was empty, what could I do? Where'd I go? I gathered up my kit, climbed the grubby steps and knocked at the door and waited . . . and waited. Silence . . I knocked again.

With a squeal the door opened a slit and I saw part of a khaki uniform.

"Yes?"

"The RTO told me to come here."

"Papers?"

I passed them through the slit and the door closed, shutting me out. I waited and my tummy rumbled sadly. Then, suddenly, the door opened again and I was whipped inside and the door shut after me. I was in the dark between the door and the blackout curtain. I fought my way out of the folds of the curtain and found myself in what was clearly an army establishment, and one, whatever the outside looked like, which was humming with life. The NCO who had opened the door to me reappeared, handed back my papers and said, predictably,

"Well, I can't **tell** you where you're going but . . . ." But she gave me a hot meal and hot water and a bed for the night and told me that tomorrow they would send me down to "our country house" in something called a shuttle.

I met the shuttle next morning, straight after breakfast, and it turned out to be nothing more exotic than a khaki-painted single-decker bus with windows completely covered with scrim, that invaluable cotton mesh that was pasted over windows to stop the glass flying about like dozens of razor blades if the window was shattered by blast.

There were a lot of other people getting on the bus, American army as well as British, but I managed to plant myself and my baggage in a seat next to a window. For a while after we started off I was too taken up with my thoughts to take much notice of where we were going. Besides, it was hard to see clearly through the scrim. But then, peering out, I realised we were crossing the Thames. A little later I began to recognise familiar landmarks and with a leap of the heart I saw that I was not far away from home.

When at last the shuttle stopped I knew where we were: we were close to Hampton Court, to be precise, in the Home Park.

The shuttle decanted me and my baggage at what turned out to be the women's camp. It housed British, American and French women, but it was predominantly American. We slept in huts and, in the American style, we ate in an all-ranks Mess. It was here, all by myself, for it was long past lunch-time, that I had my first American meal, a stupendous meal, or it seemed stupendous to me then; meat loaf with real tomato sauce and peas and corn, with a big mug of the very best coffee I had tasted for years.

In SHAEF, British personnel drew American rations, which were much more varied and generous than the British ones. I have always loved good food, and oh, how I paid for it now. Too much food, too rich in comparison with what I had been used to, played hell with my British war-time tummy. But, after a week of acute discomfort, it settled down and happily coped with a fairy-tale daily breakfast of fruit juice, hot pancakes with maple syrup and butter and large quantities of coffee with 'cream'. Never milk in that Mess. It was always cream. It certainly tasted creamy; perhaps it was evaporated milk. Sundays brought a lunch of fried chicken, which I thought terrific, even though the American orderly who dished out this special treat, lovingly reserved the rib cages for British women.

The British Cypher teams worked right round the clock in four-hour watches and there were no practice messages here. Messages poured in from the front in France, nearly always 'most immediate' and often corrupt, which means that, either through transmission difficulties or though the mistakes of hard-pressed operators, they wouldn't 'come out.' And, without the least exaggeration in the world, they were yards long. Work was at high pressure, speed and accuracy essential. Often one would have people leaning over one's shoulder, watching as the message came out in clear, word by word.

I had a bad time. Now I realised how right the army trick-cyclists had been when they suggested I should train as an army driver, and how wrong I myself had been. Cypher work is not everyone's cup of tea. The first requirement is accuracy and the second is the same. The third is unflappability. My accuracy was not high - it still isn't, and I was far too easily panicked.

Somehow I made out, more by luck than by good management, and by some miracle I avoided the Courts of Enquiry and even Courts Martial which were the fate of some operators, whose messages, wrongly or incompletely enciphered, moved troops or sent ships to wrong destinations. I found the work a fearful strain, but it was fascinating, and I liked the people I worked with and the American food was good. Also, Blitz permitting, on my

off-duty days I could catch a bus home and see my mother -
my father, too, if he was there.

By this time it was very much blitz permitting.
Germany launched the buzz bombs on Southern England
and life became dicey -or even more dicey than it had been
so far. The buzz bombs were small planes filled with
explosives and directed by an automatic pilot; they had no
crew at all on board and were literally flying bombs. They
carried just enough fuel to reach London and when that
was finished they just stopped flying, gradually lost height
and crashed - anywhere. There was no attempt to direct
the things to military targets; they were simply weapons
of terror. While they were gliding down, a puff of wind
could tip them off their course and send them to crash
miles away. Equally of course, it could send them diving
straight for you. So gently did they come down that you
could hear the wind whistling in their wings, and it was
hard to believe the destruction such small planes would
make.

Buzz bombs became a fact of life; they came daily, and
not just one or two. There were numbers of the beastly
things. They were launched from pads on the French
Channel coast, just as close to England as the Germans
could get. I suppose all the bombs were aimed, more or
less, to hit London, but, as I have said, they fell over a wide
area and south-eastern England became known as Bomb
Alley.

What I never could understand, looking back at those
times, is the complete lack of panic on the part of the civil
population, though more and more gaping holes appeared
among the rows of houses and more and more rescue
teams were brought to use their skill in digging people out
from under tons of rubble. Householders were supposed to
put notices on their gates, saying how many were inside,
but I shouldn't think it ever worked. Even in war-time one
does tend to pop in and out.

In the Home Park, with its defences and with the great thick sheet of concrete over the most important offices, we heard the alerts and now and then, when enemy aircraft were directly overhead, we took refuge under our tables, but nothing came near enough to be life-threatening, not then, at any rate.

Some light, rapid-firing anti-aircraft guns were mounted not far from our huts and, though the noise they made was simply unbearable, yet they did give us a feeling of some sort of security, so much so, in fact, that when the Americans, with their flair for the dramatic, interrupted our badly-needed sleep with their "Enemy aircraft approaching! Enemy aircraft approaching! Take cover! Take cover!" booming out from the Tannoy in the ceiling above our beds, we got to the stage of pulling our blankets over our heads to block it out and sleeping on. I went as far as curling up in a ball and putting my tin hat on top of the ball, quite sure that I was completely covered. Sleep was too important to miss, and shelters full of shrilling American women (all in their beautiful red velvet Government Issue dressing gowns) who only worked office hours, were not what we needed.

It was at this time, with the buzz bombs so bad, that I made a visit home that has stayed very clearly in my mind. It had been a quiet night for once, with hardly any disturbance at all; the guns near the huts had not fired once and I had slept really well, waking to find sunshine making its way into the hut and forming patterns on the floor. I had a feeling that something good was going to happen, but what? Then I remembered. I was off duty all day until evening. I was as free as a lark till eight o'clock.

Hands behind my head, I lay planning my precious day. I'd go over to the Mess, have some breakfast and then I'd walk over the bridge into Kingston, catch the little red bus as far as Carshalton and go home and have lunch with my mother.

Taking my canteen, that's the American equivalent of the British army mug but nearly twice as big, and my mess kit, I went across to the mess, helped myself to coffee and pancakes and found myself a place at a table. This all-ranks Mess produced marvellous food, but it did produce its surprises. Only yesterday I lined up with my mess kit behind our Senior Commander who was a peeress and in herself a great lady, when she spoke to the American orderly dishing out our lunches. She said,

"I don't seem to see any butter."

The orderly shifted her gum and turned away. Over her shoulder,

"You don't get to have no butter today" she informed our Commanding Officer, "on account you British bin naughty. You've bin parking your gum under tables and chairs like the notice says you cain't."

Ma'am looked slightly shaken as she carried her lunch to a table. As I finished my coffee and stood up, I glanced over at her - she seemed to be searching her memory.

At nine o'clock, buttons and shoes fairly twinkling, I was on my way to the gate and I was almost through it when the siren went. And almost was just not enough. The white-helmeted military policeman blocked my way.

"Not so fast, not so fast, Sergeant. Did you not hear that alert? Get into that slit trench." I stood my ground.

"I haven't time - I've got a bus to catch. I can just make it if I hurry. You wouldn't like to make me miss it, would you? There's not another one for hours."

Being a Snowdrop - or a Redcap, for that matter, is a thankless job. Show me the man who says he likes military police and I'll show you one big liar. The job toughens any man; it had toughened this one. He was immune to wheedling.

"Into the slit trench if you please, Sergeant."

I stood fast. Hanged if I'd waste my precious day in his rotten old slit trench. He could get into it himself.

But I'd been too busy arguing to notice what he had noticed, the approaching buzz bomb which took that very moment to land not far away, just outside the camp. The blast hit me and without making any move myself I found myself some feet away and standing at the bottom of the despised slit trench. Above me, the Snowdrop was just picking himself up, brushing himself down and muttering rude things about sergeants, with special emphasis on the female of the species. He went on, rather.

The All Clear sounded ten minutes later and I scrambled out and made for the gate. The Snowdrop didn't try to stop me: he seemed glad to see me go.

The bus depot was across the river, a mile or so away. By the time I reached it, hot and out of breath, it was well past the departure time for my bus, as shown in the timetable, but the bus was still there and showed no sign of leaving. The conductor joined me as I swung myself on board.

"No hurry, Sarge, two buses to leave before it's our turn. They made us wait for the All Clear. Starting early today, them buzz bombs. Looks like we're in for a narsty day."

We sat cosily in the little red bus, the conductor, the driver and a handful of passengers, swapping bomb stories while we waited to leave, and I must say, there were some really inspired liars on that bus.

Half an hour after departure time as shown in the conductor's timetable we were waved forward, the driver hoisted himself into his small cabin out in front, the conductor took up station on the step at the back, looking out and up, and we were off.

It was almost impossible to see through the windows, so thickly were they coated with scrim, but that didn't matter much. The conductor kept our destinations in his head and warned each passenger as his stop approached.

We had been going barely ten minutes and were still in the suburbs, driving between rows of houses, when the first siren went. The bus stopped, driver and conductor got out and conferred by the roadside, looking up at the sky. They came back to the bus.

"We'll go on. There's no shelter worth having round here. Bill here," said the driver, nodding at his mate, "he'll keep an eye lifting round about and behind, and I'll be watching out in front. If either of us bangs on the side, don't wait, get down between the seats, on the floor, if you can." I had the impression that the two men had done this many times before and had reduced it to a drill.

The bus ride home usually took me an hour. I have no idea how long it took that day because time lost its meaning very quickly. On seven separate occasions Bill, hanging on to the rail and leaning out, banged on the side of the bus, we squealed to a halt, the driver rolled under the bus and the rest of us cowered down on the floor between the seats, arms round our heads. Seven times huge explosions set the bus rocking on its springs. Clouds of dust and smoke crawled up into the sky beyond the houses. How many houses destroyed, I wondered, how many homeless, how many dead? What would I find when I reached home? Another cloud of dust, another shapeless pile of rubble? And mother? Resolutely, I switched off those thoughts. Take it bit by bit. Don't even think ahead.

For the last few miles I was the only passenger left. The whistle of the next bomb caught us unawares, Bill banged on the side, we streaked for a railway bridge for cover, jerked to a halt and crouched, half deafened, while a cloud of smoke and debris towered up some quarter of a mile away. Pieces of something clattered on the back of the bus. The driver leapt for his seat, the engine roared and we accelerated away . . . .

"Your stop coming up, love." said Bill, "Got yer tin 'at? That's right. Put it on. 'Ere comes another of the bastards. Run like 'ell and get under cover!"

"Thanks. 'Bye."

The little red bus pulled away and I suddenly felt lonely. I started off in a hurry; there were few houses here, and not a soul to be seen. They'd all be snug down in their shelters. I wished I were.

The noise of the buzz bomb was growing louder now, such an ordinary, familiar sound, rather like a motor bike. I increased my speed: keep going, you beast, keep going!

Only another four hundred yards and I'd be home, down in the shelter dug deep into the chalk under the lawn, not all alone in this unpopulated wilderness. I was panting and there was a stitch in my side. But, how quiet it was, all of a sudden! The motor bike noise had stopped.

I knew what that meant: the thing was falling, drifting, drifting down, the way a dead leaf falls. A puff of wind could turn it in any direction. I hurried on, glancing up at the empty sky. Where was it? Where was it? Then my ears caught the sound of its descent, the wind singing in its wings as it came slanting down to earth, and then, over the treetops I saw it, coming straight towards me. I ran.

It was like running in a nightmare when, horror unimaginable behind you, you strain every nerve to run and your feet stay rooted.

At last, the house. Through the gate. No time to fumble for a key. No use ringing. Run round the side of the house, into the garden, across the lawn, down the shelter steps - too fast, trip and slam up against the blast wall at the bottom.

The heavy timber door swung open. Mother pulled me inside, slammed the door, shot the bolts. The concussion of the explosion rocked our underground room and we held on to each other while everything danced. Dust fell on us like fine rain. Small pieces of debris clattered down on the roof of the house and we heard them slither their way down to fetch up in the gutters. The world stood still.

Mother brushed the dust from her clothes and patted her hair.

"That was a close one," she said, "I wonder where it fell. What a nasty day! But how lovely to see you, darling. When are you going back?"

CHAPTER 7

LIFE IN SHAEF

SHAEF had two sets of teams working on enciphered traffic. The Americans had their own American Codes teams, all men, and we British our own Cypher teams, mostly women. They had their offices and we had ours. We did not mix in our work. We had no access to their offices and I suppose they had no access to ours, odd really, when you remember that there were American officers on our course with us. Socially it was different; the same sort of work perhaps attracts the same sort of people, or, at least, we had a mutual sympathy for each other.

Both sets of offices were housed in the main Headquarters area, a good half mile away from the women's camp where we women ate when we were off duty, and slept whenever we could.

Both sets of offices were in a system of inter-connected Nissen huts called, aptly enough, a spider. Security-wise, it was an excellent idea; safety-wise, I'm not at all sure. What would have happened in an emergency, with only one exit, I do not know.

This entrance was guarded by Snowdrops; to get in, you had to show your pass, and the US military police were tough. They played it by the book. However well they knew you, no pass, no entry. This didn't suit me at all; it was really bad for me. My pass seemed to be constantly in my other tunic pocket, and time and time again I was taken under escort to the guard room by some towering, pot-hatted Snowdrop who was on first names terms with me on other occasions, to wait there till someone could spare the time to come over from the Cypher Office and vouch for me. The women's camp - they had a name for it; was it Camp Davies? - was so far away that I had the choice of being on time and consigned to the guard room

61

until collected - and unpopular, or late with pass and also unpopular.

Actually, there was a third alternative, if there can be such a thing. That was to cram up against the girl going in ahead of me, as we lined up to show our passes to the Snowdrop, and catch the pass she palmed back to me as she passed him. That got me in. The question was, how to get out again. No pass, no get outside again. A very literal lot, these military police, and once my saviour of the morning had passed the sentry on her way out at the end of our shift, she could hardly say a polite, "excuse me" and hand her pass to me across his well-bemedalled chest. Once I got a real stinker of a Snowdrop.

"Sorry, sergeant, I cain't let you out without I get to see your pass. How kin I tell you're not a spy?"

"Great Grief! You know I work here. How many times have I shown you my dam' pass? I've just about worn it out showing it to you. You know very well I've got one. What's the fuss?"

"Yeh, but . . See here, I know how you bin making a fool outer me when you ain't had no pass with you. I know what you bin up to. You just stay right here."

And I might have been still there, marooned in that windowless, one-exit spider if his officer hadn't arrived and heard the altercation. He said,

"You just stop tormenting my enlisted man. I know your little tricks. Just make sure that you have that pass in your hand tomorrow or you're for the guard room again and this time you'll stay there."

Rumours began to circulate about a move for us over the Channel. By this time the bridgeheads had been consolidated and the Allies were moving inland. At Caen the British were stuck, facing fierce resistance. Troops were dropped at Arnhem and at Nijmegen. I remember sending out the messages for one of those attacks, and waiting anxiously for news to come through. It was then, and for the first time, that I realised the full weight of what that very senior Intelligence Officer had meant when he told us, at Number Three Intelligence School, that we shared with the gilded staff the responsibility of sending hundreds of men to their death by one mistake. Hundreds of men did die in those operations, but the mistake was not in cypher.

Moves began: some teams were to move from headquarters to a place previously prepared, and used by Eisenhower for directing the invasion operations. They would be known as SHAEF Forward in England. The rest, those left behind in the Home Park, would gradually move over to France and take up their workload in the new headquarters to be set up just outside Paris, in Versailles.

My team was warned to prepare for the move to SHAEF Forward in England. In my next long spell off duty I snatched a quick visit home. It was the day after Thanksgiving, which the Americans had celebrated with turkey and all the trimmings and pumpkin pie to follow. I had been on night duty and when we were on that shift we went over at midnight to the British Men's Mess, which was much nearer the Cypher Office. Supper, I think the meal was meant to be. However, that mess made an unwelcome contrast to the American Women's Mess. What they did to the same rations I can't imagine, but the end results were simply not comparable. Coffee, which was ambrosial in our mess, tasted of stewed washing-up cloths over there. Nothing was delicious, the food was simply fuel. Except that turkey. It may well have been that the army cooks, trained on British army rations, were at a loss how to cope with these unaccustomed American rations, for all the British messes I ate in were good at producing traditional English food, hot and appetising - specially that cook up in the north who daily reinforced the porridge with a can of condensed milk. 'C'est magnifique, mais ce n'est pas le porridge.'

The British Mess was in the charge of a very large Cook Sergeant who had been making tentative advances to me every time I had to use his mess. Usually they took the form of extra large portions of food and visits to ask how I was enjoying it and a certain unwillingness to push off and let me get on with it. This evening we were served cold turkey, left over from the evening meal, and incautiously, I said how much I was enjoying it, and what my dear mama would give to be having such a meal.

"Your mum live near here?" he asked me.

"Yes," I said, round the turkey, "It's wonderful to be able to get over and see her."

"Going home soon, are you?"

"Yes, I'm going today, when I've had a bit of sleep." He pushed off, leaving me to eat my mountain of turkey in peace. As I left the mess, positively distended with food, he was waiting by the door;

"Liked it, did you?"

"It was lovely. Thank you very much." From behind his back he produced a large cornflakes packet, emptied of its contents and stuffed with more turkey.

"Here you are," he said, "Take this over to your mum." Completely overwhelmed, I took the packet.

"I don't know how to thank you. It's too much. Is it all right to take it?" Leaning with his hand on the wall, barring my way out from the now deserted mess, he said,

"Well, how about a little kiss? Haven't I earned one?" I did a quick dodge under his arm, corn flakes box securely gripped in both hands.

"Late. Got to fly. 'Bye."

I came off duty at eight the next morning, decided to give breakfast a miss, showered, slept till eleven, and then got up and caught the bus home, the cornflakes box held away from my uniform. It had become a bit greasy on the outside, and I didn't find the contents so attractive as they had seemed the night before. One can have too much of a good thing.

Mother didn't feel that way at all; she was delighted and began to plan how she would use it to provide meals for herself and my father.

"Are you sure you wouldn't like some yourself? I feel so greedy, taking all this from you.   How about a sandwich? I've got bread - it's not too good, but I can spare a little butter."

"No, thanks," I said, suppressing a shudder, "No, really, I'm not in the least hungry."

*   *   *

That week my team left the Home Park and went to SHAEF Forward in England.

Our new home was in Fort Purbrook, one of the string of forts built during the Napoleonic wars to protect Portsmouth.   Of the other forts, one was occupied by Combined Operations and one by 21 Army Group.

A Napoleonic fort is not quite the same thing as a modern hutted, semi-permanent camp with all modern conveniences. I never fancied exploring Fort Purbrook, but it did appear to be built into the hillside for, though our office was above ground and was reached by a drawbridge over the dry moat, most of the fort seemed to consist of miles of tunnels called galleries, and these were infested with rats. I wasn't the only one afraid to go to sleep for fear they'd attack us, and some humane Higher-up decided there would be less strain and greater efficiency if we women, just the few of us, were accommodated in tents in the dry moat.

It was delightful down there in the moat. It was quite dry; on both sides the red brick walls soared upwards and underfoot was the finest, smoothest turf. Here our few tents were pitched and we moved in very thankfully. They were the usual ridge-pole tents, with brailings, those short canvas walls that fill the space between the canvas roof and the ground, and they held just two camp beds each. We had never been so well off for space, and the weather was glorious, warm and sunny. Coming off duty, we'd go into one of the galleries where the Mess had been set up, have a quick breakfast and go to our tents. The unusually kindly Powers-That-Were had set up a few latrines for us, and half a dozen hand basins of the sort that are all in a row. Then they had considered our modesty, and erected a hessian screen all round, up to some six feet high. They even provided us with constant hot water, trundling out from some forgotten corner an ancient soya stove. This was a round, black boiler on wheels with a fire box underneath and a tall iron chimney. To ladle out the near-boiling water there were pannikins, galvanised iron scoops with wooden handles, and there we were, set up with all conveniences, if not particularly modern ones.

After a leisurely open-air scrub down, away we went to our beds, brailings fastened up, tent flaps tied back, the warm gentle breeze wafting through the tent, and sleep, wonderful sleep.

I still can't get over the unusual thoughtfulness of whoever made those arrangements for us. Up above, in the Cypher Office, life was hectic indeed, and we were all pretty stressed, so much so that my old nightmare, foreshadowed by that terrifying Staff Officer at Number Three, actually came true, though mercifully not for me. But on another shift someone did make a fearful mistake which sent a convoy to the wrong port. She stood before a Court of Enquiry, which is one less than a Court Martial. It was hard to know how they could punish her: they needed the services of every trained operator and they could hardly demote her, since by this time our War Office with its amusing ideas of economy, had reduced the rank of new operators to Corporal, while operators of the Royal Navy and Royal Air Force all held commissioned rank.

Then the Powers-That-Were had another idea: somewhere on the strength they had a small squad of
Austrians, whether prisoners of war, or people who had
been released from detention, I never knew. Whatever
could they do with these men? They couldn't join the
fighting men, they weren't used to manual labour, being
mostly professional men, and rather too old for that sort
of work. The moat was heaven-sent. They could work as
the maintenance squad down there. They could sweep and
clean, and tidy up the tents, and attend to the ablution
block and keep the soya stove burning, and collect wood
for it, light work, and well within their capabilities. So
that is what happened.

The Austrian squad were charming men, and soon
knew us all by our names. The general opinion of the
Cypher personnel was that we'd never had it so good and I
thought so too, though I was more than a little taken
aback one morning, when, having come off duty at night,
breakfasted and come to my tent, I undressed, put on my
dressing gown, went to the ablution block, filled a basin
with lovely hot water and, stark naked, was having a
wonderful wash, when a man's voice behind me, on the
other side of the hessian screen, said, most politely,

"Good morning, Sergeant Bardwell. It is a beautiful
day. May I speak with you please, when you are ready?"

None of us had ever noticed that the hessian was so
thin as to be almost transparent.

Air raids continued: when a warning sounded, the
blessed Tannoy system woke us up - if we were lucky
enough to be off duty - and we just put on dressing gowns
and slippers and shifted into the galleries till the All-
Clear; sometimes it was a long wait. It was mostly buzz
bombs that flew over but I can't remember any of them
falling in that area.

If the warning came while we were working, we just
carried on till the purple, which meant that enemy

aircraft were practically overhead, and then got down under the tables as we had done in the Home Park. I'm not sure the idea was sound; there was a load of heavy machinery on each table, not funny to have it descending upon you.

When we had settled in and were operational, the rest of the Headquarters, who had remained at the Home Park, took off for France and eventually arrived in Paris where they became SHAEF Main. They established themselves in Versailles, in the Petits Ecuries, and when they, too, were operational, our small detachment and other odd groups who had been left behind, also prepared to move forward to France.

CHAPTER 8

FAIR WIND FOR FRANCE

I was rather sorry to leave Fort Purbrook, but then, in a way, it was a relief to be doing something positive at last. Rumours had been flying around for weeks as to when we should move across the Channel, every day a fresh one. We packed again and lugged all our kit out of our tents, up through those galleries and out to the waiting trucks. That momentous summer had by now turned to autumn and the days were growing shorter and chillier.

The trucks took us away from the coast and up towards London, back to our old camp in the Home Park, but not, we were told, for long: we would be staying only until transport was available and then we would go by ship to France.

While we were still in Portsmouth I had taken a party of girls to the Naval Hospital to have our vaccinations and injections brought up to date in readiness for our departure. A few days later we went back to have typhus injections. A naval Medical Officer said, bending slightly to get down to my intellectual level,

"Now, don't you think you have made a mistake, Sergeant? Now, didn't they tell you typhoid?"

I said, feeling two feet high in the face of such august disbelief, that we had already had our typhoid shots and that we needed typhus injections, please; that I was aware that it was only needed for overseas troops, but that we were waiting to go over to France. About an hour later I began to resent that quite intensely.

The day before the confinement to barracks which always took place before an overseas move, I managed to ring my mother, and she drove over to Kingston, using her precious ration of petrol. I met her in Bentalls and we had a tea which was a shadow of their pre-war teas. I told her that I was likely to go some distance away and that, if anything happened to me she was to burn Francis's letters, that I would like her to have my jewellery, and that Francis was to have any money I had in the bank.

It was hard saying goodbye to her and I went back to camp sniffing hard. The next morning we were all confined to barracks and stayed that way till a fleet of trucks rolled into camp and we loaded our baggage and ourselves on board and said goodbye to the camp. I never saw it again - well, not for many, many years.

The trucks drove us to Southampton where we got out and found our baggage, which was whisked away to be put on board a ship. A military band was waiting for us and played as we marched to board the troopship, HMT *Cheshire*, whose captain and crew were Royal Navy personnel. We occupied the first class quarters, six of us in each cabin designed for two people. The rest of the troops embarked were mostly American replacement troops and their officers who, presumably, shared our first class quarters, though I can't remember seeing them. The troops, white and black, were accommodated in the holds.

It is not a long trip from Southampton to the Normandy coast, in miles, at any rate; this one seemed to last forever. Someone said that the ship ahead had struck a mine - I don't know whether it was true. I spent some time trying to shepherd my party from the fo'c'sle where the crew was entertaining them, quite blamelessly, with lovely thick Navy cocoa. It was all very harmless and kind, as far as I could see, but the Captain RN nearly blew a gasket. Perhaps he was used to another sort of young woman infiltrating into the crew's quarters, but however it was, I got my orders to remove the girls forthwith and sailors and girls combined in thinking that I was a rotten spoilsport and said so, and I reckoned they were right.

Apart from that, the crossing was notable for nothing, except that suddenly, in the afternoon, there was an

appalling uproar in the forward well-deck where hundreds
of American troops were gathered. The noise, a mixture of
cheering and wolf whistles, reached the bridge where the
Captain and our Senior Commander were standing. What,
he wanted to know, were her girls up to NOW? She came
down from the bridge and grabbed me, who for my sins,
was on orderly duty and in true military fashion
demanded to know what my girls were up to NOW. I said I
didn't know - not the best answer. What I didn't say was
that I feared the worst and didn't want to have a bar of it.
She barked, "Follow me!" and set off at top speed to the
first class quarters. She went rapidly from cabin to cabin,
flinging open door after door and making a rapid
inspection. All was peace and light - until we reached the
last cabin. She flung open the door and my heart went
into my boots.

Inside, the cabin was as dark as the pit. She switched
on the light, and there, filling the entire porthole, was the
khaki-clad back end of a Cypher Sergeant. Ma'am
addressed the back end,

"Come back inside this moment!" Faintly came the
answer,

"I can't. I'm stuck." She certainly was, and very
firmly, too.

Ma'am rose to the crisis,

"We'll soon sort that out! Give me a hand, Bardwell"
and with that she grabbed one khaki-clad leg, I grabbed
the other.

"All together, now, Heave!" and the culprit shot
backwards out of that porthole like a cork out of a bottle of
champagne. Through the empty porthole came a flood of
light and also a roar of disappointment, not improved by
Ma'am's thrusting out her own handsome but far from
sexy head to assess the situation. I beat a cowardly retreat,
murmuring something ill-defined about an urgent matter
I had to see to.

What passed between Ma'am and the luckless sergeant I have no idea. She worked on another shift and we saw very little of each other, in fact, the next time I remember seeing her was nearly twenty years later when we came face to face in, of all places, the market of the tiny Tanzanian town of Tabora.

At this distance I can't say whether it was the same day or the next that a Landing Craft Tanks came alongside; it must have been the next day. We were transferred over the side of *Cheshire* and into the Landing Craft's gaping iron hold. A Landing Craft must be the nearest thing to a floating bath tub ever to take to the open sea and the motion must be much the same. I'm not in the least surprised that the troops suffered so badly from seasickness on their crossing to the invasion beaches; we only had a comparatively short distance to cover and I for one was glad when it was over. We grounded on the beach, the loading ramp came down and we trooped out with our baggage and stood in a tight cluster, looking around. We had landed on Omaha Beachhead, where, four months before, the American forces had suffered terrible casualties.

It could have been some quiet beach in England. A line of low hills rose behind the beach and a row of houses faced the sea. A narrow road wound away up the hills and out of sight. And there the resemblance ended; this beach was littered with boxes and crates that seemed to have been scattered all over the sand at random, and they ranged in size from boxes that could have held a washing machine to huge affairs half the size of a house.

Of that landing only two things are really clear in my mind, the crates and hundreds of American troops sitting around waiting - didn't somebody once say that fighting a war is mostly sitting around and waiting for something to happen? - and then, as dusk crept over the beach, hundreds of tiny flickers of flame appeared as they heated their rations.

Gradually, almost imperceptibly, the numbers of troops on the beach decreased, but we sat on, empty and forlorn.   Eventually somebody appeared and went round our small group handing out boxes of 'C' rations; we opened them and dined.   The boxes contained a complete meal, with meat and semi-sweet biscuits, and also, I seem to remember, one cigarette with matches and two sheets of toilet paper.   When we finished our meal, it was almost dark and still we sat on.   Had we been completely forgotten?   Were we going to sit here all night?

The sound of engines; two or three army trucks appeared on the winding road and made their way down to the beach towards us.   We stood up, brushed ourselves down, straightened our tunics, eased our cramped legs.   We climbed into the trucks with our baggage and they drove us up and away from the beach to the Transit Camp, a vast expanse of stinking mud with a line of tents and duckboards round the perimeter.   The American Area Marshal met us and it was clear that we were less than welcome.   We should not be here.   We should be at Utah Beachhead, another landing area.   He had no accommodation suitable for women and God only knew how and when he would be able to get us away.   He was rapidly going berserk.   How, he would like to know, was he to keep us safe from harm?   Hadn't he got enough on his plate without a pack of - no, he apologised.   We must forgive him, he was under a lot of pressure.

In spite of the lack of warmth in his welcome, he found us mugs of steaming hot soup, more than welcome in an evening that had turned cold and damp and we drank it huddled round a big bonfire, the sort that reminded me of Guy Fawkes nights when I was small.   It was while we were standing drinking our soup that I noticed how deep the mud seemed to be.   The duckboards were narrow and if two people wished to pass each other, one had to step off the duckboard. I watched one soldier step down and immediately his foot disappeared beneath the mud and he went on sinking, right up to his knee, before he could haul himself back onto the duckboard and I thought of my father's nineteen months in the trenches in this same sort of mud.

The Area Marshal turned a number of officers out of their tents and put us into them and we crept, fully clothed except for shoes, into their camp beds, two to a bed, and tried to sleep.

About midnight we were roused from our shared beds and told to prepare to move: the Area Marshal considered that we were no longer safe from molestation and that he could not wait for the British trucks to arrive from Utah and drive us to Paris: we must be got away immediately and we would be transported in American trucks and he meant NOW. Apparently the black American troops had got hold of the wrong end of the stick and thought we were being entertained by the white officers and they were getting restive. He was afraid we'd all be raped - in our shared beds?

We climbed into the trucks and set off, weary, sleepy and very cold. We drove through Caen which, in the moonlight, looked like a great heap of rubble, shoulder high. Most of us were asleep when we reached Versailles early the next morning, my twenty-sixth birthday.

Our new home was in the Caserne de Croie, built by Louis XIV and unimproved since then. As far as I could make out, there were two lavatories in the whole place and they didn't work, nor did they appear to have done so for some considerable time.

The barracks were built round two courtyards. Soon after our arrival a party of American pioneer troops arrived and began to dig two deep latrines in the first courtyard and in an amazingly short time the two long buildings were erected and furnished. The amenities were discreetly separated by blackout curtains which gave a sense of privacy - to an extent. What we did until the pioneers finished their rapid improvements I really don't know.

Our new headquarters were at the Petits Ecuries, the Royal Stables, one of the two semi-circular buildings facing the Palace of Versailles. We were allocated offices, odd little eighteenth century rooms with small windows and immensely thick walls. Our equipment suddenly appeared and we were soon hard at work on the endless stream of messages coming in from the front and from England. We slept in the Caserne de Croie, washed there in freezing cold water, worked in the Ecuries and ate there in the Sergeants Mess in an immense room or hall which must once have held aristocratic accommodation for the Sun King's horses.

It was an enormous Mess, both in the size of the rooms and in the number of people who used it, navy, army and air force personnel from British, French, Polish, Belgian, even Yugoslav headquarters. The story went that soon after our arrival a spy was found, peacefully eating his lunch. It was said he was shot.

At table our meals were served by Frenchwomen from round about, most of whom were really charming. Unfortunately, others had been working for the Germans and had been rather more than friendly. French people had long memories for people like that, and when the Germans eventually pulled out of Versailles, retribution came pretty fast. Years of frustration and hatred for collaborators simply boiled over. The town had watched some French people going along with the Germans, taking money, food, clothing, even spying and ratting on their own compatriots, who were suffering a great deal of hunger and cruelty. The Germans had taken hostages at random, men and women, picked up on the street and executed by firing squad, at the rate of ten for every German soldier killed, and whole French communities were close to explosion point. With the departure of the German army the lid blew off. I don't know what happened to male collaborators, and I don't want to know, but when the avengers found women who had been friendly to the enemy and had flaunted their rewards over the townspeople, they were caught, and their heads were shaved, then and there, often in the street. It was awful to see those bare, white, egg-like skulls exposed, and, of course, it would be months before their shame could be hidden. There were few wigs to be had, and a scarf was an open admission of what it covered. Such women were branded for months.

One such woman served in our Mess and stayed unnoticed for months; I don't think she would ever have been noticed if Albert, a member of the Belgian Mission, who made one of our group who usually sat together at meals, hadn't become friendly with her and invited her to go out with him one evening for a drink. He told us all about it the next day at lunch, when somebody commented that our usual waitress was not around and a new waitress was serving us. He had taken her to a café. Things seemed to be going very nicely and Albert began to do some forward planning for the end of the evening. He put his arm around her as they sat together on the seat, and she laid her head on his shoulder. But on the wall opposite their seat was a mirror, one of those ornate things with advertisements for wine on them, and just at that moment he caught sight of their reflection.

"And, mon dieu," he told us, "what did I see? 'er 'air 'as come 'alf off! What did I do? I pick up my cap and I run! And I leave 'er to pay the bill! Why do you laugh? What is so funnee? I do not understand this British humour." Nor, looking back across this gap of years, do I; she was a pleasant woman.

Another memento of the Germans became apparent more gradually. It seems that when they realised that retreat was inevitable, they stopped treating VD cases; probably they had to evacuate too many more serious cases to have time to worry about men with self-inflicted wounds; and so VD spread among the French prostitutes, professional and amateur, and, as these ladies hastened to oblige the incoming British and American troops, the fat was well and truly in the fire. I, completely oblivious to such things, in spite of the army's best efforts to teach its young women the grubbier facts of life, knew nothing about it at all, until with my usual capacity for dropping bricks, I stated at the top of my voice one lunch time that I hadn't seen one of our group for a long time and wanted to know why he should be having such a long leave. There was an embarrassed pause, then someone said, well, he wasn't too well and was in hospital. Why, I wanted to know, what's wrong with him? It was then I was told never, never to ask such questions, that there were quite a few people with the same troubles and I could now forget all about it and be nice and tactful, if possible, when they came back to the Mess. That subdued me for quite a time.

I very much enjoyed being back in France, specially since I was pretty fluent in the language. Having the opportunity to use it every day, my French improved rapidly, till I became interpreter and general go-between between the French staff employed in the barracks and the Americans in command there. I also found out from them why, when we arrived in Versailles early that Sunday morning, instead of the smiling, welcoming faces I had expected to see in the street, there had been such black looks from the passers-by. They told me that they had been given a hard time by the German women, who had treated them with a marked lack of courtesy, and shoved to the front of queues for food and wine and things like stockings that were terribly hard to get: and, of course, paid for them with worthless money. Their opinion of them locally is best summed up in their nickname, Field Mattresses.

About this time I met a Highlander in Motor Transport who, like many Scots, had inherited a love for the 'Auld Alliance' and spoke some French. He had met a retired Colonel of Heavy Artillery, who had invited him to visit his home, where he met the Colonel's wife and young daughter. The Colonel had told him to bring any of his friends who would enjoy coming, and so he asked me. The visit was a great success, and I took an instant liking to Madame Gosselin and Marie Thérèse who was still at school. They were kindness itself to me and I came to be treated as another daughter. Madame, who spoke no English, was relieved that I could speak French, "For," she said, "it is so fatiguing, trying to make oneself understood. Now, with Jeanette, the problem does not arise." She delighted in introducing me to her friends - as Jeanette, and inviting them to guess what part of France I came from, "For, there is a slight accent, Jeanette, but of what sort I really cannot say."

She also polished up my vocabulary and pruned it of the recently acquired slang of which I was so proud.

CHAPTER 9

VERSAILLES

It was the beginning of winter when we arrived in Versailles; winters in that part of France are rather like those in London, cold and very damp. Versailles is low-lying, which probably added to the chill, and we were at the beginning of the sixth winter of the war. France had been occupied, in the north at any rate, since 1940, and the conquerors had systematically looted the country, as indeed they had every country they occupied, of everything that could add to the comfort of their own civilian population and keep the French subdued. Clothes were short; shoes, wine, and worst of all, food and fuel of all sorts. Electricity was a pale shadow of its normal peacetime strength and came and went without warning. Private cars were almost non-existent and the buses, with gas bags on their roofs, were loaded down with passengers till their rear platforms almost dragged along the ground. The Metro, well, if they didn't employ pushers to get a few more people on board, it was only because the French had had to become pretty good at it themselves.

It wasn't just France; Belgium and Holland were suffering the same way, and as winter progressed it would become worse. Insulated by my work and by the army environment in which I lived, I didn't realise how bad things were till one night, coming off duty at midnight, I turned into the American All-ranks Mess in the Caserne for supper before going to bed. As we now had our own Sergeants Mess in the Ecuries, we were required to eat there, except for these midnight snacks. The American Mess had been closed after the evening meal, but slices of ham or Spam, cheese, butter and bread, the white bread of American rations, were left for us, and there was coffee in the urn, and cream.

I helped myself to some Spam and a slice of cheese, took a piece of bread and a pat of butter, filled my canteen full of hot, creamy coffee and wandered over to a table. As I sat down, something made me look up towards a row of small, barred windows high on the outside wall of the Mess, the wall which gave on to a road. One window was open, and through it waved a forest of arms and imploring hands. I lost my appetite.

The next day, I asked some of the French women who worked around the barracks, what this was about. They told me that food was desperately short and also very expensive and that many poor people had been in the habit of searching the rubbish bins into which the mess orderlies threw any food left over. I don't understand the reason why, but the American authorities then took steps to make all such food inedible. I just can't understand why. They must have had what seemed to them a good, sound reason, a matter of hygiene, perhaps. But who cares about hygiene when people are half-starved?

I went away upset and very thoughtful, and turned the matter over and over in my mind. Then, it suddenly struck me; if there are so many people here in this garrison town so under-fed, how about the Gosselins? Are they, too, short of essentials, and yet they find coffee for me when I go round there? Have I been depriving them of food they needed for themselves? Hadn't we already been warned not to eat in any estaminets, because what food they had was for their own people?

The next time I was on late duty, after eating my own snack, I went back to the trays where food was left out for us and looked at them. All this food, I supposed, would stay here till morning and then be thrown out. There were perhaps half a dozen slices of spam, some thick slices of white bread and some pats of butter. I put them into my mess tin, the clean half. There was some cheese, too, not the real French sort of cheese, but the processed stuff. I added some of that to my pile and went up to bed.

I got up the next morning after a good seven hours' sleep and walked over to the Mess for breakfast, my mess tins, folded together and clamped shut over last night's acquisition. On my way back to the Caserne, I had to pass the entrance to the Gosselins' apartment, so I turned in. Madame Gosselin was at work in the kitchen, and I joined her there.

"Can I help?" She answered by giving me some carrots to prepare and went on making stock from some meatless bones.

"Really, Jeanette, it is becoming more and more difficult to make a decent meal for the family, and Marisette needs good nourishing food; she's growing fast, and she was so dreadfully ill last winter with an inflammation of the lungs."

"Madame," I said, hesitantly, "Last night I went into the mess for something to eat before I went to bed. I was the last one there, and some meat was left, and bread. It would have stayed out all night and been thrown away by the orderlies in the morning, so I took it. Dare I offer it to you? Would you be offended?"

I unclamped the mess tin and showed her the thick slices of Spam, the pats of butter, the slices of white bread, the cheese. She wasn't in the least affronted; she was ecstatic.

"Jeanette! The Spam! I have heard of this! It is delicious. And the butter! And cheese! And white bread! What a long time since I have seen that! Thank you so much! We shall lunch like kings! I shall cook the Spam at once. What will my husband say when he sees such a lunch?"

After that I had no qualms at all, and whenever I could I helped myself to these small left-overs which made so much difference to their rations.

My goodness, that winter was cold! Cold and damp: it seeped right into your bones. On the late shift, from eight in the evening to midnight, we'd come out of the fug of our small, ill-ventilated office, and either walk back to the Caserne or get a lift in a truck, eat a scrappy snack and go up to our rooms. I now shared a small room with two other Cypher Sergeants and it was nice to have the company, though as we were on different shifts it was rather a case of 'I'm in, she's out: she's in, I'm out.' Then, to undress, huddle into dressing gown and slippers, tramp across the first courtyard, through the archway into the outer courtyard to the deep latrines, wash in the cold, cold water in the ablution room, and scurry back to bed. Those deep latrines, how I hated them!

"Have you noticed," said Kay, who was on my shift, "something rather funny? Do you ever see an American girl in those dam' latrines?" I thought. Then I said, slowly,

"Now you mention it, I don't believe I ever do. It's not a thing you notice, really. No, I'm sure I never do. How odd!"

"Look, Joan," she said, "Next time we're on night duty, we'll do a little research. Something funny's going on. I reckon they've had some proper loos built somewhere and are keeping quiet about it. I have no intention of catching pneumonia going out to those dam' huts if there are some perfectly good loos inside under cover."

A few days later we took our turn at night duty. Relieved at eight the next morning we went down to the mess for breakfast and then came back to the Caserne, tired, yawny and ready for sleep. But first we got ready for bed; there was no rush. The Americans were just going off to work, and we waited till they had gone and the place had quietened down. You couldn't sleep till then, anyway. Then we started out on our voyage of discovery. The Caserne was a rabbit warren of small rooms and narrow passages, but we wandered on, through places we had never seen before. And then we turned a corner, opened a door and, Presto! Most beautiful, shining, spandy clean and new, a line of loos, empty and inviting, all with running water. Without a word we turned in and availed ourselves of such an invitation. The blighters, to have such a treasure beyond price and to keep it to themselves! We debated the matter. Should we broadcast our find, or should we just keep quiet and let the information gently seep through to the others? That's what we decided on. But what a difference it made to our lives! Whether there was actually hot water there or not I can't remember, though I doubt it. But that horrible trek across two courtyards in snow or sleet was over, and I don't think I ever did it again.

The weather grew colder; it was getting near Christmas. We three Cypher Sergeants found ourselves another little room. Like the other, it was small and thick-walled, with a small, barred window set into the thickness of the wall. The Sun King certainly built for permanence, if not for the comfort of his troops. But then, in the Palace around the corner, did he bother to build any loos? Loos! I had them on the brain. But what made this room more desirable was that it held a very small tortoise stove, which could be persuaded to give out heat with offerings of old letters and scraps of wood gleaned from just anywhere around the barracks and how we gleaned. Now there was often the comfort of returning to a warm room and going to bed in the warmth of the dying fire.

* * *

Even in the depths of winter the great parks of the Palace of Versailles attracted me; there were long, empty vistas, edged with leafless trees and smudgy with mist. There were lakes, there were walks with hedges like walls and adorned with statues, and the fountains! So many fountains, all different, all with their groups of statues which jetted water from all manner of unlikely places and

made complicated patterns of spray. Before the war I
believe the fountains played once a month and that was
the Day of the Great Waters, a wonderful sight. I don't
know whether in modern times the fountains are run by
electricity; if they are, that would explain why the whole
time I was in Versailles I never once saw them working.
However, there lay the Palace parks, open to all, and when
my work and living so close to people became too much, I
would take my writing case and wander off to find a quiet,
secluded place to recharge my batteries.

Then one day when two Counter-Intelligence
Sergeants from our Mess and I were all off duty they took
me to a part of the park I hadn't explored. They showed me
the Petit Trianon and the Grand Trianon, from the outside
only - they were closed 'for the duration', and then we
came to Marie Antoinette's Village. The two little palaces
looked charming and were beautiful, but the Village! - it
was tiny; among the trees little cottages with a dairy and a
fishing tower were grouped round a small lake. The
village was built for Louis XVI's queen, who was homesick
for her native Austria, and came here, so they say, to play
shepherds and shepherdesses with her friends. Poor
queen.

Madame la Colonelle, as I had learned to call Madame
Gosselin, announced that I had been invited to meet some
of her friends. Looking back on it, I think she must have
been talking about me to them, and the result was this
invitation from Madame la Commandante, who lived just
round the corner, to come for coffee one afternoon when I
was not on duty. I duly reported in to Madame la
Colonelle. I had no worries about the right thing to wear;
in army uniform I was correctly dressed for any occasion.
We walked round to Madame la Commandante's
apartment; her salon was back in use and several of her
friends were there already. It was a pleasant afternoon,
and the ladies, all wives of senior French officers, were

kindness itself to me, a mere Sergeant, and apparently had no difficulty in understanding my French. Also - and this is more difficult - I must have avoided any of those social slip-ups which are far more of a trap in another country than in one's own. Isn't it odd, that what is correct in one country can be frowned upon in another - and vice versa? The first time I saw the Colonel, napkin under his chin where it would do most good, mopping his plate with a piece of bread I was mildly surprised. Later I came to see that to leave on your plate a sauce which has been made with care and skill, may also cause a lifted eyebrow.

Madame la Commandante was farewelling a group of her friends, and I, with one eye on my watch, for I was on duty in half an hour, was waiting with Madame la Colonelle to make our own farewells. I had wandered over to a glass case of curios when Madame la Commandante returned to the salon.

"Ah, Mademoiselle, you are looking at my treasures!"

"I hope you don't mind," I said, suddenly aware that I didn't know whether it was comme il faut or not,

"I couldn't resist looking; they are so beautiful."

"They are from Egypt," she said, opening the glass case, "I went there just before the war with my dear friend, Queen Marie of Romania. We were shown all the wonderful things taken from the tombs of the kings, and we each received some small presents. Here is my favourite." She lifted from their velvet bed two earrings in pure gold. They were seahorses, their tails curving right up their backs to hook into the back of the heads. They were exquisite, perfect in every tiny detail, still fastened up. She laid one in my hand; automatically I moved to unhook it.

"No, don't open it," she said, laying her hand gently over mine, "the last person to open it was the girl who put it on when she and all her friends went to die in the king's tomb, three thousand years ago."

*   *   *

It must have been around this time that the American women's corps decided, for reasons best known to themselves, to celebrate the birthday of their corps with a march through Paris with a band and flags, the lot.

It is something I'm not keen on remembering - it's pretty paltry - but relations were not the most cordial between the two bodies of women, in fact, as far as I can remember, we had as little to do with each other as possible. Quite a bit of it may have been unacknowledged jealousy, a purely feminine jealousy. They were so beautifully outfitted; their uniforms were of such fine quality material, and so well tailored; their caps had been designed by a cunning designer who knew his stuff; their shoes had heels, and, worst of all, they wore stockings, not our khaki lisle which washed to a sickly yellow, but the new nylons about which we had heard so much, and never actually touched. They had so much kit that it was said that it took two enlisted men to move one WAC and, of course, they were much better paid than we were. Also, however they were employed, it wasn't in our sort of job and they worked office hours only.

Petty little irritations built up; they treated us as a lesser breed and we resented them, though whatever we felt had had to be carefully suppressed since our Commanding Officer - Ma'am of the troopship - had called all ATS personnel to a meeting where she had told us that whatever we felt personally, we had to be on terms of courtesy with our allies, as all branches of the Services had to be, and she would have no more complaints. It must have been awkward for her.

And now, this birthday parade. Ma'am called another meeting, this time of Cypher personnel not on duty; she asked us to join a detachment of ATS which had been detailed to march in this parade. With one voice we answered that our Sergeant's stripes were protective and we were not required to do anything outside our Cypher duties. She countered with a meanie to the effect that she knew very well she couldn't order us to do it: she could only ask for our co-operation, which she needed badly. We retired to consult our duty rosters. Some were off duty; I was on!

The unfortunate ones were now told they must learn to march in fours, something which the British Army had abandoned at the beginning of the war. Mutinously, they went on to the Place d'Armes, that huge parade ground in front of the Palace, and were duly drilled by a bemused Regimental Sergeant-major of the Brigade of Guards, who had unlearned that drill years ago.

I was off duty one morning, shortly before the parade, and decided to go into Paris to do some shopping. I waited at the corner of the Avenue du Sceau to hitch a lift with an army truck, but the first vehicle to come along was an American staff car, which stopped and asked me where I was going: I said, briefly, "Paris" and the WAC driver told me to get in. I got into the back seat indicated and we went on in sticky silence until, mindful of Ma'am's words about getting on with each other, I said,

"I hear we're to march with you in your birthday parade." The driver slowed, looked round and said, with emphasis,

"AFTER, not WITH us - with the rest of the allies."

"How nice," I said, "Just drop me here, will you? Thank you so much." The next vehicle to come along was a British three-tonner, and I climbed in, still smarting.

The Birthday dawned. With a good deal of chaffing, our team got ready for duty, leaving the others doggedly polishing up their brass. For their last rehearsal on the Place d'Armes Ma'am had handed them a large silken Union Jack with golden tassels.

"What have I got to do with this, Ma'am?"

"You're going to carry it and you're going to do it well. The RSM will show you how."

"Oh, Lor', Ma'am, must we?"

"Yes Sergeant, you certainly must."

We met in the Mess when it was all over. It had not all gone precisely according to plan. The band and those beautifully uniformed WACs with their resplendent Old Glory marched up the Champs Elysees and the French stood and watched in silence. They had had to watch many parades of foreign troops up here in the last few years. This was just another one.

Behind the American girls, after a suitable interval, came the British contingent, marching in unaccustomed fours and toting the Union Jack. Half way up the Champs Elysees somebody in the watching crowd called out, "Ah, les Anglaises! Vive les Anglaises!" And the crowd cheered.

Things were no better at the Caserne.

*   *   *

Those were the wicked old pre-'smoking-is-a-health-hazard' days; everybody smoked, and working at high pressure one was very much inclined to reach for a cigarette. It certainly seemed to help one keep calm when things were not the best. As we were with an American formation, we had no NAAFI, that odd institution of the British Services, part canteen, part corner store, part Friendly Society, but we were permitted to use the American equivalent, the PX. We received an issue of seven packs of twenty cigarettes per week at a ridiculous price, a few pence per pack. I used a few of mine and gave the rest to friends who were heavier smokers, and it was only after months of this charitable work that I understood that some of these friends had not suddenly become addicts in a big way, but were prudently selling cigarettes on the black market. The current value of a pack of twenty American cigarettes was ten shillings: my pay was in the region of thirty-five shillings a week, and I was better off than most, because the Customs and Excise by whom I was still nominally employed, made up my army pay to the level of my civilian pay. Not that that made much difference to me in France: that money was in England and stayed there, and could not be brought out of the country without any amount of complications.

But when I realised that my gifts of extra packs of cigarettes had been used in this way, I was really mad. And I think that is the only reason that I dabbled in what I knew would find no favour at all either with Francis or my father. But ten shillings a pack! And seven packs a week! I could get myself some of the luscious things in the shops in Paris, underwear, a shoulder bag, even have a little money for when all this business was over. I consulted my friends, the two Counter-Intelligence Sergeants. No trouble at all, they told me, hand them over and we'll let you have the proceeds.

So I did, and over the months I gathered a very small nest egg which came in very handy later on. This business of cigarettes was a phenomenon of the post German occupation days in France which I have never understood. It was as though the population had suddenly lost faith in their own currency's purchasing power and were looking for something else to form the basis of trade, something that would have a stable value, and somehow, they lit upon the pack of twenty cigarettes. They were not valuable as cigarettes: they were currency, with a steady buying power. I can't imagine what happened to them when they became old and tatty. But I know I bought several things which had a price expressed both in francs and as so many packs of cigarettes.

*   *   *

I made one trip into Paris with a man from the Mess who was also off duty. His name was John, I only knew him slightly; he was a good deal older than me, a shy, quiet man who had shown me photographs of his wife and small children. I took a photograph of him for her, and he took one of me, on the Alexander III bridge. We discovered that neither of us had so far visited Notre Dame, the jewel of a church on the Ile de France and we made a special trip to see it. There were few people there and we wandered round quietly, stopping wherever we felt inclined, no guides, no loud voices instructing fidgety groups. When at last we came out we found that it was later than we expected. We had intended to get some photographs as a memento and were wondering where we could get some quickly when a young woman came up to us. She was dressed in a sort of navy blue uniform, the jacket high to the neck and the skirt longer than was usual and she wore a small navy blue hat. I took her to be a Salvation Army lassie, or in some semi-religious organization. So did John. Wordlessly she held out to us some packs of picture postcards;

"Look, this is just what we need," I said, "Let's get a pack each!"

"No, I'll get a pack," he said, "and then we can look at them and if they're what we want, we can get another set from her. Otherwise we can look somewhere else when we have more time." That seemed a sensible thing to do, so, with time running short, we went to a near-by cafe and ordered coffee. While we waited, he opened the pack of post cards. The top one was a view of Notre Dame from the outside; he passed it over to me. I looked at it, laid it down, and still looking at it, held out my hand for the next one, and only when it didn't arrive did I look up. To my astonishment, his face was scarlet.

"What's the matter?" I asked, my hand still out, "Let's have the next one, John." His face still suffused, he shook his head, stuffing the whole pack higgledy-piggledy into his pocket.

"Look, don't be mean: I've only seen one."

"And that's all you're going to see. Not fit for a pig.
Come on. Back to the grindstone!" and he literally yanked
me off my chair and into the street.

It was quite a time before he managed to explain that
the pure young girl in the Salvation Army-like uniform
had sold him a pack of cards of which the first one was of
Notre Dame and the rest on quite a different subject. I
never got to see them. He threw them into a rubbish bin at
the station.

An extraordinary thing happened one afternoon,
when I was on my way back to the Caserne, and was
dawdling along, looking at the small shop windows on the
way. I suddenly became aware of odd clattering noises and
saw that all up and down the street the shopkeepers had
run out of their shops and were hooking into place the
heavy wooden shutters that covered their windows when
the shops were shut. Funny, I didn't know they had early
closing here, as they had in England. Then the jeweller,
into whose windows I had been looking, hurried out with
his shutters and said,

"Mademoiselle, hurry back to the Caserne! There is a
mutiny."

I turned to do as he said; I didn't want to get caught up
in any more trouble; I already had had enough of my own.
But before I could take more than a few steps I heard the
roar of voices and round the corner swept a mass of
French soldiers, or perhaps, soldiers of the French army
is more accurate. I took them to be from North Africa.
And right in the front, without his kepi and pushed along
anyhow by the front rank of the men was a young, fair-
haired officer. The rabble greeted me cheerfully,

"He, l'Anglaise. Ça va? Voyez notre petit officier!"

I had shrunk back against the shutters behind me. I
couldn't get any further back. But I didn't like that. I
shouted back at them,

"What are you doing to your officer?"

"We're going to hang him!"

"You can't do that!" I shouted back, suddenly brave, "You'll get hanged yourselves."

The crowd swarmed round the next corner and disappeared. I went the short distance to the Caserne, to find the imposing gateway was occupied by two American motor-bike riders, who, with their bikes parked across the entrance, were standing nobly behind them, pistols drawn. They had leather holsters slung low on the hips and tied down with thongs to their thighs; the 'US Cavalry' had arrived.

Behind them, a gang of American women enjoying every moment of these sensational happenings, sounded like a tropical aviary.

"Get behind us, Sergeant," ground out one of our protectors. "You shouldn't be out in this."

"Oh, drop dead." I replied without elegance, and went up to my room.

The mutiny, if it really was one, was never mentioned at all. Even the Gosselins didn't mention it, and I had the sense, for once, not to ask them. But what happened to the fair-haired young officer?

CHAPTER 10

THE BATTLE OF THE BULGE

Until a few days ago the actual history of the Battle of the Bulge was a closed book to me - I couldn't see the wood for the trees - I was too close to it. It is only since reading Charles B. MacDonald's massive volume on the subject that I have had any real, coherent idea of what actually happened. It is odd to realise that, when my outfit landed in France, German forces, in conditions of practically one hundred per cent security, were already massing in the Ardennes, where, according to over-confident American Intelligence, nothing ever happened.

Only today, when I laid the book down, appalled at the ferocity of the campaign and the size of the casualties, did I appreciate the gravity of the threat the breakthrough caused to the Allies.

And I also realised how Field Marshal Montgomery's abrasive personality had upset, not only a lot of British service people who came into contact with him, but also the high ranking American commanders with whom he clashed, with utter disregard both for their feelings and for the results of his insensitivity. Now I begin to understand the crowing of US servicemen over us when Eisenhower got his fourth star, and much of the ill feeling, even between the women's forces of the US and Britain. I wonder how much of the dangerous acrimony was whipped up by the media of both countries - or if it was fostered by the German propaganda machine, which had every reason to encourage a rift.

The breakout began on 16th December, and nothing seemed to be able to halt the German advance. The American army, lulled by the lack of earlier enemy activity in the Ardennes and ignoring warnings about the buildup, was unprepared.

They say it's darkest under the lamp: certainly it was so with me. At the Cypher Office in SHAEF our four-hour shifts were just work, work, work, as fast as we could go, often with people hanging over our shoulders, snatching at the messages as they came out in clear, messages so long that they had to be split up into sections for several operators to work on, to clear them as fast as possible. There was no time to ponder the contents of what came through in clear, or on what we enciphered; that was none of our concern. Ours was to do everything we could to speed communications on their way.

It was only gradually that it dawned on me that the situation in the Ardennes was more serious than the fighting that had been going on all the while in the north. It was only gradually that I became aware of the growing unease at Headquarters. This must have been when the Panzer formations were advancing rapidly and nobody knew whether they intended to make a dash for Paris or whether their objectives were Liège and ultimately the port of Antwerp.

The days before Christmas passed unnoticed. Round about Christmas Day, a lot of burning of papers took place at Headquarters; among ourselves we even giggled a bit about it and joked about our seniors getting in a flap. But it is an appalling thought that the Supreme Headquarters, with all its secrets, could have been overrun.

A few days later we were visited by an officer who proceeded to instruct us in the use of hand grenades to destroy our equipment, which, if captured, would have been a prize of immeasurable importance to the enemy, and would have compromised all our cypher communications, not only between Supreme Headquarters and commanders in every theatre of war, but also between American and British Governments. That bland instruct-ion in the use and placing of those hand grenades, eight or so at once, would, I realise now, have made it most unlikely that any of us Cypher Operators would have left that small room alive. Forty five years later, my ex-Gunner husband enquired casually if the grenades were fitted with 15-second training fuses or with 3-second battle fuses. I don't think it was mentioned.

By the end of January the battle was all over, bar the shouting. The Battle of the Bulge had been lost and won, and I suppose the survivors of those pretty little towns and hamlets were free to come back and take up life in the ruins and mourn their dead.

Of all the different wars that come to plague humanity, war in towns and villages must be the cruellest. People who want to fight a war should do what the British are rumoured to have done; hire a large, empty piece of desert and hammer it out with nobody to get hurt but the armies. No strings of refugees and their pathetic bits and pieces to be machine-gunned and bombed on the roads, no lost and bewildered children, no smashed and ruined houses, no families, shelterless, out in the freezing cold.

Back in Versailles, in the small, enclosed world of the Cypher Office, traffic slowed down a little and we had time to catch our breath. Looking back on December, I found that Christmas had slipped past almost unnoticed; the one thing that made it different from any other time was that on Christmas Eve, a Christmas service was held in the Palace chapel. It was a sort of all-varieties-get-together service and was memorable to me because George Haskin, one of the two Counter-Intelligence Sergeants with whom I had gone on several excursions, sang "He shall lead his flock" accompanied by the organ. I never knew he had such a beautiful voice, a rich baritone. Ever since then, though I must have heard that anthem dozens of times, it never fails to evoke a picture of that night in Versailles. It was bitterly cold, the town in the grip of a hard frost, the sky clear and cloudless and the moon near the full, flooding the Place d'Armes with cold light, and turning the frosty roofs of the Palace into a gigantic, sparkling wedding cake.

New Year's Day is the great day in France, and it was no different in the Gosselin household. To their great joy, their daughter, Jeanette, - Grande Jeanette, as opposed to my Petite Jeanette, suddenly appeared from the south of France, just in time to celebrate the New Year with her family.   Their son, Jean-Baptiste, was with the 'maquisards' in the bush, fighting a bitter guerrilla campaign against the Germans. They were so proud of him: from him there arrived - by some means or other - a letter and a few photographs, taken against some indeterminate background of hills and scrub. He looked tall and very handsome; I hoped all would go well with him, fighting such a dangerous war.

In spite of Jean-Baptiste's absence, or perhaps because of that long-awaited letter, the Gosselins intended this Jour de l'An to be celebrated properly. They had invited me to dine with them, but then the plan was changed. The brother of Madame la Colonelle was a Professor at the Sorbonne and the family had an apartment nearby. We were to go over to dine there with them.

We went into Paris by train and then took the Metro. The apartment was beautiful and we dined formally and in some state. The table was immensely long and there must have been at least twenty of us there. The food was a revelation, certainly in war-time Paris, where everything was in short supply, mostly because of the damage done to the railway system. For us to have had such a feast I imagine the Gosselin family must have had a farm of their own somewhere in the background.

It was late afternoon when the Colonel announced that we must be on our way, "for Petite Jeanette is on duty at eight and she must return to the Caserne before she reports for duty." What a comfort that he was somebody who understood what the army calls 'the exigencies of the Service'!

I didn't have many evenings free, but when I did, I called round to the Gosselin's apartment for a chat. The salon was shuttered and the chairs shrouded in sheets; it was far too big for them to be able to heat with fuel so hard to get. We sat in what I thought of as the 'morning room' and Madame called 'la petite pièce'. It had one of those square wood-burning stoves that throw out heat all round. This one's outside was of decorative ironwork, enamelled green, very pretty and highly efficient and we sat round the table talking, warm and cosy.

But fuel was a problem, even for such a small stove as that, and they needed the warmth so badly. I began to do a little private research: in an unused part of the Caserne I found a small dump of bits of wood, left behind, I suppose by the pioneers who carried out the sanitary improvements. I helped myself to pieces, a few at a time, just enough to be hidden in my folded greatcoat, and unloaded them on the Gosselins. It was such an economical little stove that even my contribution made a difference.

The Colonel took me one day into the salon, a high-ceilinged room, big and beautifully proportioned, and at the moment, still heavily shuttered. He opened one shutter, pushed back the heavy gold silk curtains, folded back a rug and showed me a loose board on the polished floor.

"The Boche demanded that we give up all weapons; it was death to conceal any. But I, a Colonel of Heavy Artillery, to give up even my pistol? Impossible: I loosened this board, wrapped my pistol in oiled cloths and pushed it as far as I could reach under the floorboards. Then I secured the floorboard and removed any sign that it had been disturbed. It stayed there till the day that the Boche cleared out. Oh, what a day, Jeanette, what a day! It was quite evident, you know, that they would have to retreat soon, as the Americans advanced towards Paris, but no-one could tell when. Then this night, what a noise, all night! Trucks coming and going, men marching past the house! You couldn't sleep for the noise; and then, just before dawn, all the noise died away and it was quiet, too quiet. I think everybody in Versailles must have been awake, listening.

"We got up and dressed; still not one of the usual sounds - the usual army sounds, you know, bugles, trucks, voices, men marching past. Madame and I were standing at the window - this one, keeping well behind the curtains, and so were all our neighbours, as I found out afterwards. We hear the noise of the door to the courtyard downstairs being opened, not the big door, you understand; the small one we use all the time, and there's Madame Leblanc, our concierge, out on the pavement. She looks up and down the road, turns, looks up at our windows, spreads out her hands and shrugs. She tramps off up the street, till we can't see her any more. A little old woman in black, who'd notice her? We wait and wait. Has she been arrested? Suddenly, there she is, coming at top speed - I'd never seen her go so fast, poor old soul, and as she reaches this building, she throws out both arms. Every window in the street opens, Jeanette, and she calls out - it was wonderful - "Ils ont fiché le camp, les sals Boches! They've buggered off, every one!"

*   *   *

Mail from the Middle East was coming through regularly now. Last March, when I was still at 4th Ack-Ack Group, Francis had been selected to go on an Officer Training course, and in October, about the time that I was transferring over to France, he was commissioned, passing out top of the course. It was now over four years since that last meeting at Aintree. We had written as often as we could, usually every one or two weeks, and he had sent me photographs of himself and some of the places where the Regiment had been, but now his letters began to mention something called PYTHON, of which I'd never heard. At first I thought it must be something to do with PLUTO, which was short for Pipe-Line Under The Ocean, but in later letters he explained that it was a plan to repatriate men who had served four and a half years in the Middle East. He would be due for this PYTHON in the spring.

That set me back on my heels. Francis coming home, and after all this time! For some hours I was completely happy and excited, and then the worries stepped in. What would he be like? Well, I'd had all his letters - he couldn't be so very different. But what would he really be like? Would I know him? Of course I would. I'd got his photographs, hadn't I? But, his voice? I couldn't sort of hear it, however I tried. Then, again, we were both four years older, and what a four years it had been for both of us, packed with the sort of experiences that made it much more than four ordinary years. Would he like me when he saw me? Perhaps he'd think I was plain, uninteresting; the Middle East was probably packed with sloe-eyed houris, specially the Western Desert, where he'd spent so much time. I began to work myself up into one of my famous 'tizzies' that the trick cyclists in Lancaster must have detected.

Bearing in mind the nature of my work, and the state of mind into which I had worked myself, it was bound to happen: I made a blob in a message and did the job thoroughly. Nobody loved me and I was up before an embarrassed Major.

"What's the matter with you, gel?" he boomed at me from the safety of the other side of his desk. "Never done this before, eh? Can't do this sort of thing, y'know. Bad show!" I nodded miserably. "What's the matter with you, eh? Something wrong?"

To my horror, tears filled my eyes and rolled down my face. I heard a wobbly voice saying,

"My fiancé's coming home on PYTHON and he wants to get married straight away."

Looking uncomfortable, the Major cleared his throat:

"Should be delighted: nothing to cry about. Jolly good show."

"But I haven't seen him for four and a half years," I wailed.

He came out from the shelter of his desk, patted me gingerly on the arm as though it was hot, bolted back behind his desk, and said,

"Thought there must be something. Shouldn't worry if I were you. Wait till you see the whites of the eyes. Sure it'll be all right: not a flash in the pan - four and a half years! Now off you go like a good girl and take a bit of extra care, eh? Off you go."

That was all the wigging I got, a good deal less than I deserved.

Every day the American Post Office in the barracks, which dealt with mail for all women living there, put up a list of names of people who had parcels waiting for them. I rarely bothered to look; I wasn't expecting any parcels, and we certainly neither wanted nor needed food to be sent from home. So I was mildly surprised to be told that there was something addressed to me in the post office and I'd better pick it up before it was posted undeliverable.

It was from Francis, and contained lengths of the most beautiful fine silk, yards of it, some white and some black. The accompanying letter told me that he knew I wouldn't be able to have any wedding finery, nor a trousseau, come to that, but perhaps I could have this material made into sets of underwear.

When in doubt, seek expert advice. I repacked the parcel and went to see Madame Gosselin; she was in the petite pièce, looking doubtfully at some very worn bed linen, which she thought of turning sides to middle. With some relief she put the sheet down.

"What have you there, Jeanette? It looks interesting." I laid the parcel on the table and opened it;

"Francis has sent this to be made up into lingerie; we can't buy things like this in England. What should I do?" She lifted the white silk out of its wrappings.

"Very nice. A good quality. Your fiancé has excellent taste, I see. This, I think, should go to my lingerie maker; she will provide the lace - like other unimportant things, there's still plenty of that in the country. She can make it up into petticoats and knickers. She will make them entirely by hand. Ecru lace, I think." She lifted out a smaller packet, white silk chiffon. "Just enough for a blouse: she will also do that." Laying aside the white chiffon, her eye fell on the last packet, the black silk chiffon; she opened it. "Tiens!" she said, and that was all for a full minute, while I stood guiltily beside her, feeling my face grow hot with embarrassment. At last she said, "I do not understand why it is that English gentlemen should wish their brides to be dressed in clothes better suited to the demi-monde."

But she forgave me the lapses of my inexplicable nation and took me to visit her chemisière, who lived in a tiny, blue-shuttered house quite close to the chateau. She was received like visiting royalty and I realised, probably for the first time, that in this garrison town, she would go pretty high up the social scale. Madame set about ordering my trousseau in a business-like manner, explaining just what was needed. I was measured, pattern books brought out and the most suitable ones selected. Through it all, the two French women proceeded serenely, consulting each other over my head, very much as if I had been, in fact, a daughter of the house.

In an incredibly short time Francis's silk was converted into the loveliest underwear I have ever owned, every stitch done by hand, and delivered in layer upon layer of tissue paper. Madame examined every garment minutely, and at last said, that yes, they would do, in fact, she would go so far as to say that they were very nice, and 'convenable'. I don't think she meant the black ones.

More and more I was absorbed into the Gosselin household. I became aware of the worries, the deep anxieties that underlay their cheerful kindliness, little things in normal times, mountains in these days. Shortages of essentials, like shoes. Marisette's shoes were wearing out: the Colonel cut up his uniform belt and mended them with strips of its leather. I wrote home to my mother, and she sent me a pair of shoes I had bought just before I went into the army. They were a bit big for Marisette, but with the hand-knitted cotton stockings Frenchwomen were wearing, they did quite well. My father wrote to the Colonel, thanking him for their great kindness to me; the Colonel wrote back to him, assuring him that I was well and that they were doing their best to take my parents' place, that all was well with me. It was about this time that I first noticed the care with which they surrounded me. If I visited them in the evening, when it was time to return to the Caserne, the Colonel would say, "Ah, Jeanette, permit me to accompany you; a little walk will do me good." He escorted me the few hundred yards to the gates of the Caserne, not stopping until he delivered me to the Orderly Room, just inside the entrance.

I was touched by his care for me, but a little puzzled at the same time: it was such a short walk. But then I began to see what I hadn't noticed before. American soldiers, bringing their dates back to the Caserne, were saying goodnight to them and all along the pavement on both sides of the entrance were couples locked in each others arms. He was scandalized, and very upset that I should be exposed to such sights. It was wrong for a well-brought-up young woman to see such behaviour. "Ne regardez pas,

Jeanette, ne regardez pas!" he would say, hurrying me past, "Don't look! Whatever would your father say?"

* * *

If I thought that my very mild wigging from the Major was all that would happen to me after my messing up a message in cypher, I was wrong. The mills of the cypher world didn't grind particularly fast but they didn't let blobs like that one get through without at least a bit of a polish up. As I was collecting my cap and bag to go off duty, the Officer of the Watch came over and said to me,

"By the way, you're down for a week's refresher course, starting next Monday. Contact RSM Dunne, will you? He's taking the course and he'll arrange transport."

Well, that's it, I thought, my chickens are coming home to roost. Ah, well, there's nothing to be done. But when I climbed up into a three-tonner the following week and found some ten other operators already on board, the course took on a faintly holiday atmosphere. Most of the others were men - did they make more mistakes than women, or was this, after all, not a form of defaulters' parade? We drove out of the part of Versailles I knew and eventually swung into a wide drive, and as we entered I saw a large notice, L'ECOLE DU GENIE - The School of Engineers.

And here for a week we were truly put through our paces by RSM Dunne, a brilliant teacher who made that refresher course a pleasure. He also was the owner of the most beautiful speaking voice - he came from Fife, 'the Kingdom', as he told me, and he assured me that in Fife the only pure English was spoken.

We spent the mornings being lectured about various aspects of cypher and doing exercises and then returned to the Ecuries for lunch. There may have been more than our course going on at the Ecole du Genie, for members of my course tended to arrive piecemeal. One afternoon I came back in a personnel truck without the canvas cover on the back. As we came up the main drive to the school, I saw several of the men on my course standing in a line behind a low wall a few yards off the drive. I waved and called out, "Hi!"

To my amazement, with one accord they ducked down and vanished behind the low wall. How strange. Whatever was the matter with them?

They arrived not long after me, and I said,

"Well, you're a miserable lot. I waved to you, and you all ducked and didn't answer."

One of them said,

"Young Joan, when you get a bit older you'll know when to turn a polite blind eye. That was a gentlemen's urinal, and your friends on the course were all very occupied."

I was mortified.

So mortified, in fact, that I refrained from asking anyone what they thought of a mural on the wall behind RSM Dunne's head. I sat and looked at it for a week. It was a picture done, I imagine, by a German soldier, of a small boat drifting down a river, which, from the amount of hills and castles on each side, must have been meant to be the Rhine. In the boat were a soldier and a girl. Neither of them appeared to have any control over the boat, nor did they appear to have any interest in where they were going, which struck me as unwise. The soldier was saying something to the girl in what I supposed was German, but though I had done a year or so of German at school, these words were not in my vocabulary. I decided to play safe and not ask; after all, they could have been Arabic.

At the end of the course, refreshed, I was returned to the bosom of my team and life continued comparatively uneventfully.

CHAPTER 11

PYTHON

Francis was now stationed at the Royal Artillery Base Depot at Almaza, near Cairo, and letters both ways arrived much more quickly.

Each letter that came said the same thing; it wouldn't be long now before his PYTHON leave was due and then he'd be on his way back to England. That was as specific as he dared to be, and after all these years of censored mail and 'Be like Dad, keep Mum!' I didn't expect precise information. Work kept me busy, and life was pleasant enough; the Gosselins were so very kind to me and I was able to make occasional trips into Paris. And when I felt that things were getting on top of me, there was always the blessed quiet and solitude of the Village, with its silent little cottages and tower, and the calm lake.

The one incident that broke the comparative peace of those days was the mishap that happened to our old friend, Albert, the Albert of the lady with the wig. He was one of those charming creatures who run headlong from one crisis to another. We saw him most days in the Mess and always there was some 'histoire' for him to tell, but for the last week nobody had set eyes on him; perhaps he had gone on leave. But this day, he came into the Mess walking stiffly, and there was a film star bandage round his head. Somehow, it didn't make us feel sympathetic; he simply looked rather more raffish than usual, with his fair hair curling theatrically over the top of it.

We gave him a cheery welcome:

"Hello! What have you been doing? Checking for wigs?" He sat down gingerly, screwing up his face with pain.

"Poor Albert, he's been wounded; Where've you been? Crossing the Rhine single-handed?"

He shook his head carefully,

"No, my dear friends, do not laugh at your poor Albert. He is in big trouble. I am needing much sympathy, please: do not mock at me."

The story, when we got it, interspersed with sighs of pain, was pure Albert. It seems that somebody had brought to Versailles the open touring car owned by Field Marshal Göring, an enormous white Mercedes-Benz, and parked near Albert's office. Albert, seeing it, and as usual, acting first and thinking afterwards, had a sudden urge to drive the thing. He ran downstairs to the car. The keys were in the lock; he hopped in and switched on the engine, which caught straight away and he drove off. It was only when he needed to make a sudden stop that he found that the great car had no brakes, none at all. He hit a wall . . . .

February went past slowly. Surely spring must be getting close, and this cold, damp weather give way to warmer days. Paris in the spring! It made me think of sunny days, sitting in street cafes over cups of coffee, watching the world pass by, hats sillier even than those the French had concocted to keep their morale up, skirts even shorter, and those ridiculous hand-knitted white stockings. Also, it was getting very difficult to scrounge wood for that tiny stove in la petite pièce. I wished so much that spring would come.

March. The cold hung on grimly though the trees were beginning to show that lovely tender veil of green, a promise that winter was nearly over.

At the front, the race for the Rhine was on, and Patton's Third Army was careering across country faster than seemed possible. Again, what I knew of it was from other people; I was too busy concentrating on my work to have any idea what was in the messages that went through my hands. And spring was really in the air now - once or twice I went over to the mess without my greatcoat.

On Sunday, 17th March I was off duty till lunch time. I improved the shining hour by going to Mass at St. Louis the Martyr, came out and turned my steps towards the Rue de l'Orangerie and the Gosselin's apartment. I was nearly there when I saw a Sergeant from the Orderly Room coming towards me; she waved, and I stopped.

"Where have you been?" she asked, "I've been hunting everywhere for you. The Senior Commander wants you straight away."

"Do you know what she wants me for?" The eternal question - what have I done - or not done?

"No, I've no idea, but she wants you as soon as possible."

"Thanks. I'll go straight away." Whatever could it be? Not a Cypher matter - that would be dealt with by Cypher personnel. How very odd. I reached the Orderly Room, and said to the Corporal at the desk,

"The Senior Commander wants to see me."

"Yes, that's right. I'll tell her you're here." She was back in a moment:

"You can go in." I went in, saluted and said,

"You wanted me, Ma'am?"

"Yes, Bardwell," she said, "You'd better sit down." I took off my cap and sat on the edge of a chair. Something must be wrong.

"Bardwell," she said, "I have some news for you. Your fiancé ." She paused and the long-awaited nightmare descended on me. Out of the nightmare I heard my voice saying,

"He's dead. Thank you, Ma'am." I got up blindly from the chair. She came round her desk and took hold of me:

"No, he's not - he's alive and well and he's already in the UK. He had a quick trip home by sea. He wants you to join him."

That broke me up in pieces. I wept, and the most astonishing thing was that her arms were round me and I was making the front of her beautiful tunic wet with my tears. I think she cried, too.

Then, realising that this was not quite according to King's Regulations, I wiped my eyes, tried to apologise, but she said, "I think we could both do with a cigarette, don't you?" and offered me her case.

She had just received a teleprint from Francis's Commanding Officer, Colonel Mansergh, an old friend of hers. She showed it to me: it read, 'Prospective bridegroom on high seas. Please expedite bride.' Hard on the heels of that message had come another saying that he had arrived in England and wanted me to join him.

"You'll have six weeks' leave with him" she said, "we can't do much about a plane today; how about going tomorrow morning?"

"Yes," I said, "that would be fine - - - no, Ma'am: I'd like to go to Elizabeth Arden in the Place Vendôme tomorrow and get tidied up. Could I leave on Tuesday?"

"Of course," she said, "so that's arranged, Tuesday morning. I'll have you informed of the time. It'll probably be early."

Lizzie Arden was so kind to Service women; somehow she always managed to fit them into her busy salons and give them an hour of luxury, wrapped in pale pink, fluffy blankets, so unlike our own grey army ones.

The next morning I hitched a lift into Paris in an army three-tonner and arrived at Elizabeth Arden's and soon I was wrapped in those pink, cloudy blankets and feeling every moment more and more like a girl going to meet her fiancé and less and less like an army Sergeant off duty.

I was lucky enough to catch a lift from the Place Vendôme almost straight away, and a jeep took me all the way back to the Ecuries. I thanked the driver and started off down the Rue de l'Orangerie towards the Caserne, but as I reached the door to the Gosselins' apartment, I suddenly realised that with all the excitement I had not had time to tell them my news. I turned in, called, "La porte, si vous plait" to Madame Leblanc lurking in her dark cave at the side of the big street doors. She clicked open the door to the staircase, and I ran up the stairs to the Gosselins' apartment. Madame Gosselin was alone in the kitchen, preparing lunch; Marisette was at school and M. le Colonel was visiting an old comrade in arms.

"Chère Madame," I said, reaching for a potato to peel, "such excitement. Francis has returned from the Middle East and has reached England. He has six weeks' leave and he wants me back straight away. I am to fly tomorrow, and my Commanding Officer told me that I shall have six weeks' leave, too. It seems that she received two messages about it, one when he left Egypt and one when he reached England and they both arrived together."

Madame embraced me warmly:

"That is good news, Jeanette, and Monsieur le Lieutenant has reached England safely, in spite of all the dangers of the sea. How long will it be before the lawyers will be able to arrange the marriage settlement? They must hurry, so that you can be married and spend a long leave together."

For a whole minute I couldn't think what to say: how could I break the news that in my shiftless country nobody bothered about marriage settlements unless large sums of money and big holdings of property were involved?

"I am afraid," I said, carefully, "that among people in my parents' circle it is unusual for a formal settlement to be drawn up. I do have my dowry (this was quite true) but apart from that, there will be no other formality." I waited in dread for the coming remark, and it came:

"Tiens!" said Madame Gosselin, and the subject, in front of me at any rate, was closed.

The next morning I had just breakfasted and packed my bag when the Orderly Room sent to tell me that the Command truck was waiting. It was a sort of monster jeep, open of course, and we made the airfield in record time, with me clinging on to my cap with both hands.

I was flying for the first time. The plane was one of those Dakotas, DC3s, beloved by so many Service people. It was unheated, unpressurised, and they certainly didn't serve meals or drinks, but we did have proper seats. I didn't appreciate that distinction at the time, but I did later. After the first few minutes, when I had managed to swallow my heart which had unaccountably lodged in my throat, I realised I was the only non-commissioned person on board. There was a lot of gold braid about, several men who could only be Admirals, and quite a few high-ranking officers with Staff tabs.

Also, in the seat in front of me was a very handsome officer, a Colonel, who had a delightful speaking voice. When he turned sideways on to me I recognised that profile: it was David Niven.

The Dakota landed at Croydon Airport, and mundanely, after travelling in such company, I caught a bus to Carshalton Beeches.

To say that my Mama was surprised to see me is an understatement. Of course I had not been able to let her know I was coming - I'd hardly had time to collect my own wits.

"Where's Francis?" I asked, as soon as I decently could.

"My dear, we had no idea you could be here so quickly: he's gone down to Devon to see his mother. He only left this morning."

That was a really hard blow. I had come so far, all keyed up with expectation that he'd be there when I arrived, and now I still had to wait. I swallowed my disappointment and settled down to enjoy being with my parents and at home again. That in itself was wonderful.

Francis rang the next day, and we talked on the phone. Most of what I had to say was just, "Oh, Francis." But he seemed to understand.

We decided that he should stay with his mother for a few more days and then I should go down and join them. Accommodation was difficult in the West Country, as so many people had left the South-East because of the bombing and were staying there more or less permanently in hotels. And, as well as that, the country was crammed with Allied troops, most of whom appeared to be visiting Devon. Francis, however, managed to arrange for a room for me at his hotel, and that was a relief.

I left home on the Thursday and went down to Devon. With every mile I grew more anxious about our meeting. It was such a long time, four and a half years, since we had seen each other. What would he think of me? Had we both changed? I took a deep breath and steadied myself as the train ran into Dawlish station, slowed and stopped.

I stood up, took down from the rack my case, respirator and tin hat, my bag, the usual junk, and climbed down from the train. Behind me the train made preparatory noises and began to move off. It gained speed and the last carriages whisked past me with a puff of dusty wind. The platform had cleared: it was empty save for a single officer. I stood still because my legs wouldn't go any further.

It was Francis: taller, thinner, sunburnt, but still Francis. For a moment nothing seemed to move. Across the distance between us we just looked at each other. Then his arms opened and so fast I don't remember moving, I ran into them, dropping case, bag, respirator, tin hat unnoticed on the platform. His arms closed round me hard, my face against his chest. A singing joy welled up from deep inside me and I knew, without any shadow of doubt, that all was well, that all would be well. The two halves split asunder for so long, had come together again, the golden thread was still there unbroken. It had never been broken. The four and a half years were nothing: essentially we had never been apart.

He released me, produced a spotless handkerchief and mopped my face, removing tears and careful make-up. He gathered up my things from the platform and handed them to me, picked up my case, held out his hand and said, "Come, darling." With a hand under my elbow he guided me to the gate. On the way, he said, casually,

"Oh, by the way, I've got a special licence: I thought we might get married before Easter. It doesn't give us much time, but that doesn't matter, does it?"

"Not at all," I said, "It doesn't matter a bit."

*   *   *

We spent the rest of the week in Devon and then on the following Monday morning the three of us, Francis, his mother and I, went up to London by train. His mother went to stay with friends; Francis stayed with us. That Monday was the Monday of Holy Week, a time when marriages are not usually celebrated, and the earliest we could be married was the Thursday, Maundy Thursday, the day before Good Friday. The Parish Priest looked a bit disgusted that we should wish to be married at such a time, but during the war there was a general slackening of the rules for Service people, and married we were.

Francis's best man was Desmond Burgess, a friend of his from the Yeomanry, and the brother of a school friend of mine. My dear Mama had managed to arrange for a wedding cake to be made: she had been saving ration points for just such an emergency. Hardly anybody we knew was still living at home - they were either away in the forces, or away doing civilian jobs, or just away, bomb dodging, so it looked as if our wedding would hardly be the social event of the year. As it turned out, about twelve of my family's friends were able to come and a few of Francis's.

I had bought a new uniform cap from Moss Bros. for the occasion - something old, something new, and my wedding outfit was in a popular tone of khaki, donated by the War Office. I spent a few traumatic moments in my bedroom, trying to decide whether the old cap (issue) or new one (Moss Bros.) looked worse, threw one on the bed, where it promptly fell between the bed and the wall, so that I had to spend precious time crawling under the bed to retrieve it, while my father was calling to ask whether I intended to go to my wedding today or tomorrow. I crammed on the one I'd rescued - it was the new Moss Bros. one - and dashed down the stairs and into the car. Half way to the church I remembered I'd not polished my shoes and spent the rest of the trip rubbing my shoes in turn on the backs of my stockings.

Arriving at the church - it was raining - I pulled down my tunic, straightened myself and got as far as the door into the church. Up the long aisle I could see Francis's red head. Suddenly I panicked.

"My God," I whispered to Daddy, "I can't!"

"My God, you CAN!" muttered my father, "I've got you this far: now IN you go!" He put his hand on my back and gave me a smart shove, and I must be the only bride on record who entered the church and started up the aisle at a trot.

By the time we reached the altar steps there were two men in service dress standing waiting. I thought their Sam Brownes looked very well polished; that was as high as I dared look. In fact, I might have been married to the wrong one for all I would have known, until the end of the ceremony when Francis kissed me.

After the reception we were driven to London in a large limousine with white ribbons, but after we had gone a mile or two, Francis called to the chauffeur to stop and the ribbons were removed; then we finished the journey comfortably private.

The West Country hotels were crowded; we had been quite unable to find anywhere else to stay for our honeymoon, but the hotel where we had been staying in Dawlish offered us, rather apologetically, a basement flat - sitting room, bedroom and bathroom. The rooms we had formerly occupied had been booked a long time ago and this was all they could offer. We were delighted. All newly-married people must crave privacy more than anything and we had so much to talk about, to learn about the intervening years, to re-learn about each other, that our own little flat was ideal.

At breakfast the next day the other guests, who had known us before we went up to London for the wedding, came over to our table and congratulated us. One elderly couple, obviously devoted to each other, gave us a piece of advice. The man, a retired Colonial Governor, said: "Whatever happens, always be kind to each other." What better advice could there be?

We must have spent nearly a month down in Devon. We went out all day almost every day, walking up on Dartmoor or wandering round the places Francis had known when he was a boy on holiday with his parents. We visited Buckfast Abbey, stayed while the monks sang Vespers, such beautiful, passionless plain chant. One day we went up to Bovey Tracey, to visit his great-aunt at Hummersknott. She received us in the octagonal drawing room, a lovely room in the centre of the house, with a great octagonal skylight set in the ceiling. Great-aunt Amy was a tiny woman with a crown of piled-up white hair. Francis introduced me to her:

"Aunt Amy, this is my wife, Joan; she has just come over from France."

A pair of needle-sharp blue eyes surveyed me, like twin laser beams, and in her precise little voice she asked,

"Are you a French lady?" It was evident that French ladies were not particularly high on her table of favourite

Joan Bardwell at
Ide Hill, Kent
27th August 1939

Joan with Francis
at Blackpool
January 1940

II

Francis during the
Battle of Britain,
September 1940

Joan , Blackpool,
Winter 1940-41

ATS in AA Command, on an operational gun position

ATS operating an AA height/range finder

Francis in Asmara
Eritrea, June 1941

Joan in Paris,
winter 1944-45

Francis, Cairo, winter 1944-45

Francis and Joan in wedding dress, Dawlish, March 1945

Francis in Devon
April 1945

Joan in Devon
April 1945

Francis and Joan, Bad Oeynhausen, June 1945

Francis with half-track, Hartz Mountains, winter 1945-46

Joan, Hastings, 1946

Francis and Joan,
Hastings, 1946

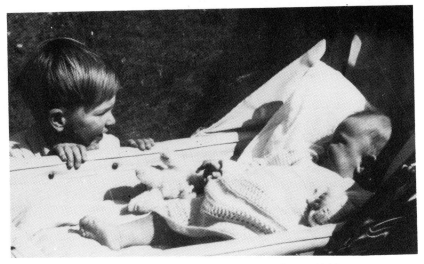

Christopher and Rosemary, Torphins, 1948

Torphins, looking to the south-east
View of front of Mrs Anderson's and of prefabs in background

Torphins, looking to the north-west
Photos by courtesy of the *The Press and Journal* of Aberdeen

Joan, Torphins, 1946

Joan and Christopher in Woodside Crescent, winter 1946-47

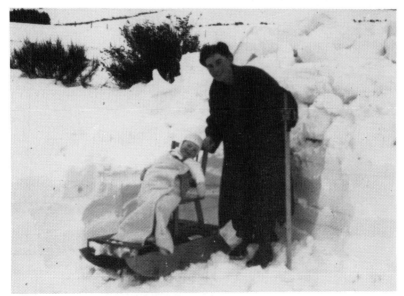

Joan and Christopher at the end of a road, winter 1946-47

Christopher and
the first bee hive,
Torphins, 1947

Christopher,
Torphins, 1948

Christopher on Daddy's motor bike

Rosemary in the Dunkley Duchess

Joan and Francis with Rosemary and Christopher,
Torphins 1948

people. I made haste to mutter that I was stationed in France, but that really I was true-blue British. She seemed relieved.

So quickly those precious weeks passed. Secretly, inside myself, I ticked them off. One day, he would say to me, "On Monday" - or Tuesday, or some other day - "I must report back to RA Depot at Woolwich" and I would have to say, "And I must go back to Versailles" but not yet, not yet.

The week, the day, came. We went back to London. I went with him to the station, another station, and watched another train pulling out. Would it never end? Was I always to be left desolate, watching a train going further and further away?

Well, I was alone again: he had gone; only as far as Woolwich, at present. And I must gather my thoughts together for my own return to Versailles. There was the question of what to take back for the Gosselins. Pure coffee, that was the first thing; mother spared me a can of Spam, and I found another pair of shoes I'd bought just before I went into the army. They would do for Marisette. What else? I can't remember. Only a large section of wedding cake. With those in my bag, and with the usual tin hat, respirator, shoulder bag - recently issued; the War Office had just awakened to the fact that women were accustomed to carrying their bits and pieces in bags, not in trouser pockets - I said goodbye to my father and mother and reported back to the elusive Bryanston Square.

Going through Customs on my way to the plane, I was rather thrown when the Preventive Officer asked me if I had anything to declare. I said, with a modest simper, that I had some wedding cake, and he passed me through.

Versailles felt strange after so long away from it, but I settled in; I had some difficulty in answering to my new name, but that passed.

CHAPTER 12

THE LAST STAGES

It was the end of April when I returned to the small world of Cypher. Spring had come and the trees in the Palace park were in full leaf, the pale, delicate colour of young foliage. There was still a nip in the air; a photograph taken then shows me wearing my woollen gloves and, over them, a pair of khaki fingerless mittens that my Mama had knitted for me. By the same post she also sent me a most peculiar pair of khaki socks to wear over my stockings. They were knitted in a spiral stitch, and the heels were just wherever my own heels happened to be, very good for darkish mornings when I had snuggled in bed till the last possible moment.

But, thank goodness, greatcoats, heavy things, were a thing of the past.

The armies, both British and American, had long since crossed the Rhine and were moving forward at a tremendous rate; General (Two-gun) Patton had taken a photograph of the 200,000th German prisoner of war entering the cage. Mussolini was dead and Hitler killed himself on 30th April. Surely the surrender of the German armed forces must come soon.

It came on the 8th May, 1945. It is quite impossible to explain what that meant. The war had spared nobody, man, woman or child. Now there would be no more fighting, no more bombs, no more shells. Peace. And Vera Lynn's lights could go on again all over the world - well, over Europe, at any rate. It was unbelievable.

I was due to go on duty at eight that evening; I spent the morning writing to Francis in my favourite place in the Village, packed up my writing things and went back to the Mess for lunch, and then with a few friends went by train into Paris, to see the fun.

In Paris the streets were already crowded, and I was glad that we had a few hefty men to help us through to the George V Hotel, which was set aside for British troops. From its high windows I looked down into the streets at the crowds, people dancing, strangers embracing, men weeping. Peace, my friend, it's all over. No more fighting! No more Occupation! No more killing of the Boche in dark alleys, no more hostages taken off the streets! No more firing squads for hostages. It's over. Fini!

It was before six that evening that I said to one of the men - the same man who had bought the pack of photographs at Notre Dame - that I'd better be getting back to Versailles; it would be slow work getting to the station through the crowds and we didn't know what the trains would be like. He said at once that he would go back with me; he'd seen all he wanted and things were due to get out of hand.

We worked our way to the station through the happy crowds; on the way I was hugged and kissed more than ever in my life. It didn't matter who or what you were - your uniform represented the liberators of la Belle France.

The train for Versailles was standing in the station, and it was packed already: obviously a lot of people thought this was the prudent time to go home. We climbed in; there was space by the door to stand, and we stood there, exchanging pleasantries with other passengers.

Suddenly, there was a well-know dreadful sound, the high screaming of a dive-bomber right overhead. Automatically, I hit the floor, arms round my head, hands clasped over the back of my neck. As I fell, I had a glimpse of my companion doing the same thing. Tense, I waited for the explosion . . . and waited.

I opened my eyes, raised my head from the grubby floor: looking down at our prostrate bodies was the tight group of our fellow travellers, smiling kindly. "Don't be afraid, la petite," said a man in black beret and collarless shirt, "It's only the 'blue birds'; they have to show how happy they are!" The 'blue birds' were members of the French Air Force, and I should have enjoyed my trip back to Versailles much more if they had shown their happiness in some other way.

We got to our feet sheepishly, brushing dirt and dust and the remains of French cigarette stubs from our fronts and spent the rest of the journey trying to look as if it had never happened.

In the Cypher Room there was little traffic that night: I expect the armies were so glad of a respite that they couldn't even take it in that there would be no more fighting. The end was too sudden, the transformation from war and death to peace too great. It would take time to sink in.

Cypher traffic picked up, and life went on as before, but with differences: The Gosselins' son, Jean-Baptiste, appeared out of the fastness of the Maquis, on leave, just as handsome as in his photographs, and with extraordinary tales to tell about the fighting his resistance group had been doing. I began to wonder about civilian life, life as a married woman. Surely Francis would not want to go back to the bank - it seemed ludicrous to imagine him dishing out money in a small, stuffy bank. Well, we'd leave that bridge until we reached it; there was no sign that things would change for some time.

*   *   *

After Francis had been at RA Base Depot a few days he received a posting; it was to a regiment in Wales. He set off at once, full of enthusiasm.

His new regiment, however, puzzled him. It was a Field Regiment, like the one in which he had spent so many years, but with a difference; it seemed to be some sort of holding or transit regiment, made up of men and officers from all manner of artillery regiments. Some officers, like him, were back after years of service overseas; some, officers and men alike, had never been in action. The result was a lack of the feeling of unity which is such an important part of a regiment's morale. Francis felt unsettled; this was not his sort of place and I was still in France. He made up his mind, and six weeks after his arrival in Wales he applied for a posting overseas again, to Europe.

*   *   *

At the beginning of June I went past the door of the Signals Office on my way to the Cypher Room just as a Signals Sergeant came out, carrying some papers.

"Lucky you!," she said, "Off on leave again. You're only just back. How do you fix it? I wouldn't mind some leave myself."

"I'm not going on leave," I said, "I've had nearly six weeks. I shan't get any more for ages." She held out a teleprint.

"Have a look at this, I'm just taking it to the Cypher Room." I took it and read the message, clear and unquestionable, that I was to be returned to the UK forthwith for two weeks' embarkation leave with my husband.

"What on earth is this about?" I asked blankly; "I don't know anything about it - it must be a mistake."

"Wish they'd make a mistake like that with my leave!" and she whipped ahead of me and knocked at the Cypher Room door. I followed more slowly.

The news was broken to me more formally by the Officer of the Watch, who informed me that my husband was going on embarkation leave and that she was obliged by regulations to send me to be with him. I had the impression that if it had been anything to do with her, I'd have been sitting hard at work and not gallivanting all over Europe again, leaving the team short-handed.

So it was, that, for the second time in three months I found myself in a DC3 on my way to England, and not at all sure what it was all about. This time I was not travelling with the top brass: this plane was a troop carrier and fitted with two metal benches, one on each side, that ran the length of the plane. Overhead were the fittings for parachutes to be hitched on to. It was like nothing so much as one of those old trams of my childhood, and we sat and swayed in unison, in exactly the same way as a tram-full of passengers. The only difference was that trams do not usually hit air pockets.

This time, when I reached home, Francis was already there. I said,

"What's this embarkation leave? Where are you going?"

"I couldn't stand that place," he said, "I'm joining a regiment in Germany; we'll be nearer to each other."

He explained then, about the uncomfortable atmosphere of the regiment in Wales and the lack of regimental spirit. Then, he said,

"The end came when I went over to the Mess and found some WAAF girls playing strip poker with some of the officers. The girls looked as though they had been losing quite heavily. I went back to my room and applied for a posting to Europe. There was some surprise at my applying to go overseas again so soon after my tour in the Middle East, but when I said that you were in SHAEF, my application went though straight away."

"That's wonderful," I said, "SHAEF will be going forward into Germany soon - or, at least, that's the rumour."

"I thought we might go to the Wye Valley for this leave," said Francis, "I've managed to book a room in a small hotel in Hereford - I don't know what it will be like. I thought we should take our bikes with us on the train: we can use them to see the countryside. It's really beautiful down there."

The weather down in Herefordshire was beautiful; for the whole two weeks it was fine and sunny. The little old hotel was far from smart, but it served; we had a comfortable room and every day they packed us some sandwiches and we took off for a day's wandering round the country on our bikes. And the bikes had needed a little refurbishing; mine had been hung up in the garage for three years, Francis's for six.

We had two wonderful weeks; Versailles ceased to exist, Cypher ceased to exist. There was not much traffic on the roads - petrol was scarce and strictly rationed, and cycling was a pleasure. We visited Ross-on-Wye and photographed the ancient Market House. We took a funny little two-coach train that wandered down the Wye valley; the scenery was superb. We went and saw the suspension bridge over the Severn, and Francis told me that a Yeomanry Officer he knew had been invited to leave the RAF before the war for flying his plane under the bridge.

We had a little difficulty at first in remembering to ride on the left side of the road, and were reproved very gently by a traffic policeman at a crossroads in Hereford, for coming up from behind him on his right side.

We went to Tintern Abbey and wandered about trying to piece together what it must have looked like. There was nobody there but us and the wind made sad noises among the ruins.

And somewhere in the Malverns we visited some ancient British fortifications on the top of a hill, the earthworks so old and yet indelibly stamped into the ground.

But the most vivid memory of all was not of ancient buildings, but of cycling along a road between fields of beans in flower, making the air full of their scent. I've never smelled it since: you miss so much in a car.

The last few days came; reluctantly we put our bikes in the guard's van and travelled back to London. I reported to

Bryanston Square and a little while later was on another DC3, another troop carrier with tin seats, winging my way back to Versailles and the world of Cypher.

*   *   *

At Versailles all was not as it had been when I left for England, two weeks before: the place was humming like a hive.

"My goodness, you picked a fine time to go on leave again," said the Officer of the Watch as she passed with an armful of documents, "I don't suppose you've heard the news. We're moving forward in a fortnight's time."

"That's short notice, Ma'am, where are we going?"

"As far as I know, to Frankfurt-am-Main. That's where SHAEF will make its home, in the I.G. Farben complex, and we shall stay with them until the time comes for us to go up to the British zone." I wondered when that would be.

But the more I thought about it the less I liked it. I should have to say goodbye to the Gosselins, who had loomed so large in my life ever since I arrived in France. They were more like family than friends. As for Germany, I couldn't think of one pleasant aspect of being stationed there.

That feeling was strengthened a few days later, when we were given a lecture on our coming move and told that there would be absolutely no 'fraternising': it was absolutely forbidden. At this late time I can't remember what the definition of 'fraternisation' was, but we were given to understand that there would not be even conversation with the German population.

I said a very sad farewell to the Gosselins; I could never thank them enough for all their great kindnesses to me. I had brought them more coffee and some canned fruit in my baggage when I flew back, but what good was that? Luckily, transport was improving now and supplies would be moving a little more freely.

Early one morning we left from Villacoublay airfield. The plane was another DC3 troop carrier with the usual tin benches and overhead fittings. By the time we were all on board, the benches were full and then our kit was brought on board and stacked in a long mound down the centre between the two benches. There was a lot of it, and it filled the space so well, that, when the air crew came on board, they crawled over the mound to reach the cockpit. We took off.

We had been in the air perhaps ten minutes when I smelled smoke. It grew stronger and stronger. The plane filled up with smoke. Through the window on the other side, the starboard side, I could see flames. One of the engines was on fire.

Nobody said a word, nobody moved, but we must have all been as taut as springs. A lot of people began to cough uncontrollably as the fumes caught their breath. I didn't cough: I was fighting a violent urge to be sick. We lost height rapidly and at last touched down on an airfield.

"Everybody outside! Quick!"

We didn't need telling: coughing and spluttering we crowded out and sat on the ground, taking deep breaths of clean air. I have no idea what happened to the plane; presumably the ground crew put the fire out, but we waited, sitting on the ground for some time. Then the flight of Mosquitos who were based on that field, came back and had a delightful time buzzing us.

At last the crew came back and told us we could all get back into the plane; the engine was not damaged and the fumes had cleared away. Apparently somebody had stuffed the engine with newspapers.

It was a hot day and very bumpy, and we had to cross mountains, either the Ardennes or the Vosges. The plane jolted and twisted, and dropped suddenly in air pockets. It was all too much for quite a number of girls: two buckets appeared, one to each bench, and these were passed up and down the line for contributions. I did not contribute, but I had the most awful headache I ever remember. On and on went that flight as though it would never stop, and I could hardly believe it when we began to lose height and came down at an airfield. It was Frankfurt-am-Main.

We crawled out of the plane and lay down on the grass. I never wanted to move again, ever. I'd just lie here till I died and I hoped that wouldn't be long. We must have lain there a good half hour before an officer - I didn't know her - started on us like a sheepdog, and we crawled to our feet. Trucks had arrived and we and our kit were put on board and driven to a number of blocks of workers' flats of the most excruciating ugliness, part of the I.G. Farben set-up. They were like monstrous shoe boxes, all exactly alike, and their ugliness was made even worse by the fact that they and the I.G. Farben office complex they adjoined were the only things left standing in acres and acres of rubble. Nothing apart from the I.G. Farben seemed to be more than ten feet high, the whole city just a jumble of debris, which choked even the roads, so that there was barely room for a truck to work its way along.

At one of these blocks of workers' flat our truck stopped and we were decanted and left to move in. The flats were all empty, the owners having presumably been evacuated or left to get away from the bombing. They were still more or less furnished and were for us to sleep and rest in only; a Mess had been set up for us in the Headquarters building itself, and our Cypher Office had also been set up there and was ready to start operating.

The flat to which I and another Cypher sergeant were assigned was small, just a single living room, a bedroom with two metal beds, a tiny kitchen and a rudimentary bathroom. We dumped our kit in the bedroom and looked round. Well, it was a roof over our heads, and we didn't have to spend more time in it than necessary. I certainly wouldn't want to. Every bit of furniture had been painted by a very amateur hand and the colour chosen was a screaming yellow ochre, except where areas of the original dark brown paint showed through. We stood silently for a minute, looking around, then Margaret said,

"Yes, well, I think the Mess, don't you?"   And we went.

CHAPTER 13

FRANKFURT

Life in Germany was in sharp contrast to my very pleasant life in France. In those early days of the Occupation the ban on 'fraternization' was absolute, so that we British, and even more so, we of the British Cypher team, were thrown into each others' company rather too much, with small chance of getting away from the military scene and none of having non-military friends, as I had had in France.

Of course, in the nature of things, that total ban on fraternization couldn't last: it had to be relaxed, and eventually it was, though by that time I myself had returned to England. Pity alone would have brought about its relaxation for life had become so dreadfully hard for the defeated. And life for the British troops had become claustrophobic and that wasn't good for morale.

Cypher was a job that made heavy demands on us, not so much physically as mentally. Today that would be recognised as stress. Whatever the high head ones thought it was, the War Office had decided, even before D-Day, that eighteen months was the longest that any cypher operator should be expected to work in our conditions. After that we might not be so reliable or would show some signs of strain. I had worked at Cypher a good deal more than the War Office's eighteen months, and one of my friends, a Staff Sergeant who had been with SHAEF since before D-Day, had already been sent back to England to rest.

It was just then, when we were all a little jittery and feeling that nasty cooped-up feeling, that some idiot of a Member of Parliament back in England stood up in the Commons and made a fatuous speech about our 'gallant girls going forward into Germany' and then added what was, in our view, a colossal insult, "They will be such a comfort to the troops." That tore it. The bastard! What did he think we were? What did he think we spent our time doing?

In the teleprinter room, which sent and received all our work, there was a girl called Ailene. She was no dumb cookie. That girl had everything: she was a first rate operator, she was pretty, blonde and had a lovely soprano voice and a wicked sense of humour. I'd known her for ages. One afternoon we met as I was going on duty and she was on her way to the Signals Office. We talked about this silly MP. "See!" she said in her Lancashire voice, "If only I could get my hands on that man! Well, I can't, can I? But I've made up a song."

After all these years I can't remember much of it, but it went to the tune of John Brown's Body and started:
"Have you heard the latest story?
There's a job we have to do.
It isn't what we joined up for.
And we think its time you knew.
They are sending us to Germany,
But not to see the view,
They're sending us as comforts for the troops."
and the chorus ran:
"Oh, whatever will me Mum say,
Oh, whatever will me Mum say,
Oh, whatever will me Mum say,
When she knows that I'm a comfort for the troops?"

That song went all over the ATS and it expressed our outrage. It wasn't just what the silly fellow had said: it was his utter ignorance, after so many years of war, of the immense part played by the women's forces, or of how many of us had been killed or wounded. In his job he had no right to be so ignorant.

We sang Ailene's song; it was a good marching song, and we added it to our repertoire which contained such gems as:

"She'll be coming round the mountains when she comes."

and the second verse:

"She'll be wearing khaki bloomers when she comes."

It was Ailene, too, who composed that delicious song to a male Quartermaster Sergeant, who, of course dealt with all our clothing needs, and this one was to the tune of that well known aria from Samson and Delilah,

"Oh, Love, from thy store let me borrow
One pair of khaki pants to wear.
One pair of cotton stockings or else
My little feet will have to go bare."

Poor Quartermaster Sergeants! They had a thin time at the hands of the ATS. Our lisle (cotton) stockings began life a decent khaki, but with repeated washings they faded until they finished up a sickly yellow. It was not to be borne, but a wheedling visit to the QMS was met with,

"There's nothing wrong with them: you'll have to go on wearing them until they're worn out - AND when I can see that you've tried to mend them." The army's rule was that Q could only hand out clothing as replacement, so the worn garments had to be handed over in exchange.

Fair enough. Now, how to wear them out quickly? It took a little experimenting, but at last a method was perfected. You borrowed a razor blade from some soldier you knew, and then sat and gently, very gently, you stroked your knee area with it. Gradually, soft fluff appeared; you blew it away and continued. The stocking got thinner and thinner, all over the knee area. Put down the blade, give a quick sharp bend to your knee, and the whole stocking, thin as silk, suddenly gave way, in a great hole, with countless ladders running up and down. Now the other leg.

I'm sure he suspected some evil doing. Quartermasters always suspected the worst. Their theme song, when approached for any of their precious stores seemed to be, "Push off: ain't got none!" or words to that effect. But whatever this one thought, he never managed to prove anything.

But the worst job the Q had to do with the ATS, and one that must have cut his frugal heart to the core, was the handing out of sanitary towels on demand. This not only went against the grain, but was embarrassing, too. Poor Q: how he must have yearned to go back to his own safely all-male regiment.

There's a nice tale told about those bunnies and every member of the ATS will swear to its truth. Early on in the war, when girls were first conscripted into the forces, Lord Nuffield, the immensely rich head of the Morris car firm, said to the woman who was head of the ATS,

"I want to do something for these brave girls of yours, something that they can all share in. It doesn't matter what it costs! Money doesn't enter into it. Now, what do you think they'd like?"

"You'd really like to do something big for them?"

"That's right."

"Something they'd all bless you for?"

"That's just what I want to do."

"I can think of one thing - but it might cost rather too much."

"Anything!"

"Are you quite sure? I mean . . ."

"Absolutely, my dear lady, absolutely."

"Right! You can provide sanitary towels for them all."

And he did, too, and they were bunnies of the very best quality, though the gift was one that he could hardly cause to be trumpeted abroad.

*   *   *

Somehow I couldn't settle in Frankfurt: I missed Francis, I missed my French friends and to top it all I felt far from well. I had picked up some tummy trouble, which refused to go away.

Also I found that, in spite of myself, a distinct change in my attitude to my job had taken place. Information had arrived from the War Office that married women could now apply to be demobilized. The war was over, the urgency of the past was gone. If I made a mistake in a message, so what? If they didn't like it, they could do the other thing. I wasn't just their Cypher Sergeant to order about: I was the wife of Lieutenant F.G. Smith, RA, and what were they going to do about that?

My tummy trouble still plagued me, and I had started to be sick as well, bouts occurring at any time during the day and night. My uniform skirt was getting quite loose, so I must have been losing weight.

With the cessation of hostilities we were not nearly so busy in the Cypher Office, so we took on a few of the administrative duties we had been excused before. One evening I was Orderly Sergeant to a Junior Commander whom I had never spoken to before, Mrs Hirschberg, an older woman with white hair. When I had finished what I had to do, I reported to her in her quarters. She looked at me hard and said,

"You know, you're not looking as well as you did. Are you all right?"

I said that I had a tiresome tummy upset and was being sick a lot.

"Have you seen the MO?"

"No, I hate doctors: I'll be all right. It'll go away, I expect."

"You got married recently, didn't you? Aren't you the girl whose fiancé came home on PYTHON?"

"Yes, Ma'am, that's right. I'm just back from two weeks' embarkation leave. My husband is joining an artillery regiment in the British Zone."

"And you're being sick all the time? My dear, do you think by any chance you're going to have a baby?" I looked at her in horror:

"Oh, my goodness! I can't be." Gently she asked me several questions, and then said:

"I think it's quite possible that you are. Where's your husband now?"

"He's stuck in Liège, waiting for the regiment to send transport for him: they are moving out of what is going to be the Russian Zone back into the British Zone. I don't know where they'll be stationed."

"Liège;" she mused, "I imagine you wouldn't mind seeing him and telling him the news."

"That would be marvellous, but how?"

"Oh, my dear," she said, "there are empty planes going up every day to Brussels. Try and hitch a lift. I would. I'll make sure you get a forty-eight hour pass."

"Thank you very much, Ma'am. Good night."

I went back to my quarters with a good deal to think about. What an extraordinary thing! It hadn't even crossed my mind. I managed to get into touch with Francis with the unofficial help of the Signals Office, making the call in one of the vast rooms filled with machinery. The line was terrible, but the engineers boosted the sound and eventually we could hear each other, shouting above the din of static. He promised me that if I could make it to Brussels he would be there to meet me. He didn't ask any questions, but he just sounded warm and reliable. That was the first step, at any rate.

As I was going off duty next day, the Officer of the Watch came over to me: she handed me a forty-eight-hour pass:

"Mrs Hirschberg told me you wanted to have a talk with your husband in Brussels. Here's a pass - I hope you manage to get a lift." I began to thank her but she said,

"There's just one thing: it's quite likely that we shall be making our move to the British Zone the day after your pass expires, so, whatever you do, don't get delayed, or you'll arrive back here to find we've gone."

I thanked her, promised to be back on time and went back to that small I.G. Farben worker's flat that I shared with Margaret. It was odd about the I.G. Farben complex. As I have said, the whole of Frankfurt seemed to have been devastated, the roads choked with fallen walls and rubble, but alone amidst the destruction, the I.G. Farben complex of buildings and its attendant shoebox blocks of workers' flats, was almost untouched. Only one block had been hit by a bomb and that was at the extreme end of the building. The rest of the block looked all right. The general opinion was that the complex had been spared deliberately to become the headquarters of the American Zone.

The following day I went on duty at midnight and worked until eight the next morning. I went straight back to the depressing little flat and slept for a good four hours, waking up refreshed and ready for action. I dressed, packed my overnight bag, checked that my pass was in my top left-hand pocket, along with my pay-book, my AB64, and set out for the RAF airfield. It wasn't far.

I found the RAF equivalent of the Orderly Room and went in. A corporal sitting at the desk said "Yes?" in an discouraging voice. I said, hesitantly, that I was hoping to get a lift up to Brussels. Had they a plane going that way? He gave me a look of dislike, picked up a pen and said,

"Name?" I gave it.

"Number?" I gave it.

"Rank?"

"Surely you can see."

"Sergeant. Religion?" I gave it.

"Next of kin?"

"My God, Corporal, I'm not wanting to join your outfit, just to hitch a ride in an empty plane." It made no difference. Poker-faced he held out his hand:

"Pass?" I gave up, handed it over.

With a glint of triumph in his eyes he handed it back, "Yes, well, we've no planes going just now. Come back this evening."

"Thank you so much," I said, with all the sweetness I could muster. Now, Joan, don't bang the door as you go out; you may have to come back.

I marched out of the RAF gates and crossed the road to the US field, found their equivalent of our Orderly Room and went in. Another corporal was at this desk, lying back, almost horizontal in his chair. Without moving, he sketched a salute, surveyed me with a lazy grin and said,

"Hi, sugar. What do you want in this den of iniquity?"

"I'm trying to get a lift up to Brussels. I've asked the RAF, but they haven't anything at all going that way."

"Well," he said, "I guess you're the lucky girl. There's a DC3 due for take-off in a few minutes." He extricated himself from his chair, walked over to the door, and pointed across the tarmac.

"See that plane getting ready to leave? Just go and talk pretty to the pilot. He'll take you. No worries."

"Don't you want my name? Number? Next of kin?"

"Not a thing, sugar. Happy landings!"

I went and talked pretty to the pilot. All he said was: "Hop aboard. There's a couple of GIs in there. We'll have a cup of coffee when we're good and airborne."

We did, too, though it was a little difficult to manage my cup in the air pockets. It was a bit difficult to manage my tummy, too, but I made it.

It was a bumpy journey and I was glad when we lost height and the navigator said briefly, "Brussels!"

For the last half hour I had been wondering what I would do if I couldn't find Francis when I reached the airport, but in all that sea of khaki he was the first person I saw. We greeted each other with a careful lack of display.

"Come along," he said, picking up my bag, "I've got a room in an hotel reserved for British troops; it's old-fashioned and rather nice and I've booked us seats at the theatre this evening. Don't know what it'll be like - all in French, I expect."

When we reached the hotel he took me up to our room and sat me down on the enormous downy bed.

"Now," he said, "tell me all about it: what's gone wrong? Are they expelling you for being a naughty girl? Or is it just a court-martial?"

I shuddered:

"For goodness' sake, don't make rotten jokes about things like that!"

"Well, then, love, what's wrong?"

"I think I'm going to have a baby." I blurted, watching his face.

"Well, isn't that splendid?" He gave me a hug, "I was hoping that would happen."

"You were?"

"Yes, you've had quite enough of the army; time you got out and had a rest. You can get used to being a civilian again."

That settled that small thing very satisfactorily. We dined together very happily, with no interruptions from my tummy, walked to the theatre which had put on a sort of Folies Bergères, and then strolled back to our hotel.

Bearing in mind what the Officer of the Watch had said about missing the bus, we arrived at the airport next morning in very good time. If it had been crowded yesterday, this morning the place was packed, and I was told by the Transport Officer that for some reason all Air Force planes, both British and American, were grounded.

There was no way that I could get a plane back to Frankfurt.

My God! The Move!.

"Now, look," said Francis firmly, "there's no sense getting yourself upset yet. Just hold your horses, will you, and sit down while I see what I can do."

He sat me firmly on the last square inches of a crowded bench and disappeared into the milling khaki mob. I perched there miserably, clutching my bag and wondering what the penalty would be for missing the move.

He was back, sooner than I expected, with a Transport Officer in tow. It appeared that there was just one plane leaving for Frankfurt: it was not an Air Force plane, but a small Avro Anson, loaded with medical stores and heading for Czechoslovakia. The pilot was a woman Ferry Pilot, a sort of semi-civilian. He led us out on to the tarmac where this small plane was standing, ready for take-off. The pilot, a blonde girl with long, curly hair, wearing a navy sort of uniform with woolly dolls on the lapel, said to me,

"I've got 14 kilos weight to spare: that should be all right. Let's get going."

The entire fuselage of the plane was packed with bales, leaving a space of about two feet under the ceiling. She said,

"Sorry there aren't any seats - we had to take them out. Can you lie on the top of the bales?" I crawled over and settled myself. So far, so good. I hoped my tummy would think so, too. We started up the runway. The plane took a long run before we were airborne, and it gained height sluggishly, but we rose in time to miss the fence at the end of the runway. Luckily I couldn't see what Francis saw.

This plane carried its aerial along underneath the fuselage. Whether it should have been retracted, or whether it was in its right position I have no idea. As the plane rose, the aerial caught on the fence . . .

I made myself comfortable on the bales, and now that the trauma of getting transport was over I relaxed and drifted off to sleep.

I must have slept for some time: when I woke, the little plane was droning on its way, the pilot was giving her long, blond hair a thorough brushing and combing and in the intervals, calling up some station on her radio. She didn't seem to be getting any replies. She turned round, and seeing me awake, said,

"Goodness, you must have been tired! You've been asleep for ages. We're not far from Frankfurt. I don't know what's the matter with them: I keep on calling them, but they don't reply."

We flew on. Looking down I saw we were approaching a great area of devastation. Frankfurt. The pilot began to circle. We circled and circled. She looked round again.

"I can't think what's the matter with them: I keep on asking for permission to land, and they're firing rockets at me to tell me to go away! I've got to land soon to refuel!"

"Is the radio working?" I asked.

"It was all right in Brussels before we took off: I used it to speak to the tower. If I can't land here, we'll have to go on to Wiesbaden. Will that be all right for you?"

"I expect so," I said doubtfully. Where on earth was Wiesbaden?

We landed safely, and it was only then that she discovered what had happened to the aerial. I left her to it. I had seen the millionth chance - a big staff car, the sort that is used to transport generals and other delicate goods. It could only be from Frankfurt.

So I returned in style, and was greeted with open arms, for nobody believed I could possibly get back from Brussels: Frankfurt had been deluged with rain, and the airfields, both of them, were flooded.

CHAPTER 14

BRITISH ZONE

It was as well that I got back to Frankfurt when I did: the MOVE was on next day. I went along to the Cypher Office to pick up some things I had left there; the place looked very forlorn, all the equipment already packed and gone and just a few bits of packing material and scraps of paper were lying on the benches and floor. I was about to go out when I heard the sound of marching feet. I looked at my watch; it was one minute to six. I went to the window and, for the last time, watched the small ceremony of the lowering of the flags.

On the terrace below stood two flagstaffs, side by side; on one the Stars and Stripes, Old Glory, moved lazily in the evening air. On the other, the Union Jack moved in harmony with it.

Round the corner came the flag party, a few white-helmeted, white-gloved US military policemen and a bugler; behind them, as well-turned-out, two Redcaps, British military policemen. They marched to the flag staffs, two US men to Old Glory, the two Redcaps to the Union Jack. As the minute hand of my watch moved to the hour, the bugler raised his bugle and sounded the Retreat, and, as it sounded, slowly, smoothly, in perfect time with each other, the two flags came down; the four men unfastened them and folded them. A word of command, they stepped back into their places and the flag party marched away, round the corner and out of sight.

That was the last lowering of the Union Jack in Frankfurt. Next day, the flagstaff would be empty, and Old Glory would fly all alone. I picked up my bits and pieces from where they lay among the shavings and went out of the room, leaving the door open. There was no need to close and lock it any more.

Our leaving Frankfurt, though low key, was in fact, marked by no less a person than General Eisenhower himself, Uncle Ike to all his troops.

Now that the fighting was over, medals were being awarded to the deserving. Each of the men in the American Codes Office received a medal for his service, and Uncle Ike asked Field Marshal Montgomery to allow the British Cypher Teams to receive the same medal. Montgomery pointed out that British troops were not permitted to receive decorations from anyone but the Sovereign. So that was that. Still un-bemedalled among the clanking hundreds of Americans, we felt naked, yet we had done no less than the American men.

But our Uncle Ike wasn't finished yet; instead of a medal we each received a Citation, a small piece of thick paper, beautifully printed, setting out our contribution to the successful conclusion of the war.

I lost mine.

*   *   *

The British Cypher Teams moved out of Frankfurt the next morning in three-ton trucks, fitted, as on my very first day in the army, with benches on each side, and we drove north through Germany. I have only the haziest memories of the drive, long as it was; my tummy, after a few days' comparative peace and quiet, was showing signs of non-cooperation, and I dreaded the journey. But, at any rate, the weather was fine and we could have a delightful drive through the countryside.

From the map, it looks as if it would be about 250 km from Frankfurt to Bad Oeynhausen, where 21 Army Group Headquarters was established, but maps are little to go by. Dozens of bridges had been destroyed, miles of roads made impassible. What route we took I have no idea, but the whole way we never once saw a town, only the countryside, rich and mellow in the heat of summer.

It was late afternoon when we drove into Bad Oeynhausen, a smallish, pretty town, unharmed, as far as I could see, by the war and, as its name suggests, a town catering for visitors who came to drink the waters and to bathe in them.

Houses had been allocated to us, probably guest houses in normal times, and we settled in very comfortably. I shared a room with Maggy May, my friend, and I thought the move would have its good points. At least I was out of that depressing flat, with the crudely daubed yellow paint over all the bedroom furniture.

The next day we had no duties: we could rest, go for walks, find the park, the Kurhaus, where the waters and baths were, do what we liked. I went round to the Mess, just round the corner from my house, tried to eat some breakfast, tasted the first margarine I'd faced since 4th Ack-Ack days, was told by the orderly that she was sorry, the coffee had run out, but how about a nice cup of tea, decided I couldn't cope and went into the ante room, where I found a sofa and lay down, feeling very delicate. I slept.

I was awakened by a little voice, saying, "Sergeant! Sergeant! Wake up!" I came up from somewhere deep, deep down, opened my eyes and found one of the Mess Orderlies standing beside me. "Sergeant!" she said again.

I came fully awake:

"I'm sorry, I must have dozed off. What is it?" She looked a trifle scared:

"There are two officers outside and they're asking for you."

"Who are they? What do they want?"

She shook her head,

"They didn't say, just asked if you'd arrived."

"Ask them to come in, please."

She turned and disappeared. I shut my eyes again. When I opened them Francis was standing beside me. Francis!

He had been waiting in Liège for transport, day after day. Before the cessation of hostilities, the regiment to which he had been posted, the 32nd Field Regiment RA, had advanced well to the east of the line which was now to be the boundary between the British and Russian Zones of Occupation. Accordingly, the Regiment had to move back to its new position on the British side of the Zone Boundary. This new position was in the Hartz Mountains. Until that was completed there was no transport available to pick up one officer stranded in Liège.

Headquarters 21 Army Group
and from August 1945
H. Q. British Army of the Rhine

At last a 15-cwt truck, driven by a Lieut. Jones, came and picked him up and when Francis told him that his wife was due to arrive in Bad Oeynhausen, he announced that it was hardly out of their way, and so there they both were and did I think there was any possibility that they might be invited to stay for lunch?

Charm will get you anywhere; they lunched with me, and then they, Maggy May and I went on a tour of Bad Oeynhausen. It was just as well that Lieut. Jones knew the place a great deal better than we did, for neither Maggy May nor I had done any exploring except from the house to the Mess. We sat in the park and took photographs of each other, and talked till Lieut. Jones said they'd better be starting on their way, for the roads were bad and he wanted to get in before dark. The regiment was now stationed in the small town of Osterode.

I felt much happier now that I knew Francis was not too far away. It was obvious that I was ill; I was still losing weight and the vomiting went on day and night. Our new Cypher Office did little to help: the Post Office building, which was the home of Signals and Cypher, was a neo-Georgian building of red brick, with two square blocks of offices joined by a long, narrow block. The Cypher Office was at the top of one block and the loos were in the corresponding position in the other. Each time I had to be let out of the locked room to run across the roof of the middle block, down into the end block and so to the loos. On my return I did the journey in reverse, and knocked at the door of the Cypher Office for somebody to let me in. Then one day in the Mess my skirt nearly fell off - I just caught it as it slipped. I cannot think where a nappy pin could have come from, but that's what someone gave me; I folded the fastening of my skirt right over to fit and pinned it securely.

At last I agreed to go to the MO. This was a young woman, straight out from England and very self important. She questioned me abruptly and with no courtesy at all and I resented it and said so. In the middle of a slight scene I was grabbed by a bout of sickness while the sergeant looked after me and comforted me. When it was over the MO asked in the voice of one revolted beyond endurance:

"Do you do that much?"

"All the time." I said shortly and marched out. Francis, who had driven over on some errand, was waiting for me and I told him that I would never go back to that woman.

"I'll go and have a word with her," he said, but I wouldn't let him.

But somehow, the news that I had seen the MO and been treated badly reached my Officer of the Watch, and she asked me about it. I told her, for I was really hurt, that she had treated me as if I disgusted her and I was sorry, but I just couldn't take any more. She asked me why I had not told her before: it seemed that there had been other complaints.

"Try to hold on a little longer," she said, "I have an idea things are going to change."

They were all so kind to me, even when I flew over the roof with boring regularity and did nothing like my share of the work. Then Francis started coming into Bad Oeynhausen regularly. One of his regimental duties was taking truck-loads of Displaced Persons from the United Nations Relief and Rehabilitation Administration (UNRRA) camp at Osterode to another UNRRA camp well to the west of Bad Oeynhausen to start them on their way back to their own countries. These poor people had been forcibly taken from their homes in occupied countries and sent all over Germany to work as slave labour. Now, half-starved and far from their own countries, and with the railway systems of Germany and France almost obliterated, they were to be returned to their homes. There were thousands of these poor unfortunates, speaking French, Dutch, Polish, Belgian, Russian - they were the ones treated worst of all. It was a tower of Babel.

At least I had adequate French for most occasions. With that and a smattering of German, Spanish and Russian I was a step ahead of Francis, and he began to call in on Bad Oeynhausen on his way, to pick me up, so that I could translate for him. If nobody could tell them what was happening, they saw themselves being loaded into trucks and driven off to some unknown place and, with their experiences of the Germans, they expected an extermination camp, or a mass killing in the forest. I myself didn't realise just what terror could grip a load of DP's until one day as we started off after a roadside halt, Francis left the hand brake slightly on. After we'd gone a distance, the brake shoes began to smoke and the smoke drifted up into the back of the truck. We heard the shouts and screams and Francis pulled up and ran back to see what was the matter. They were beside themselves with fear, thinking they were to be gassed. I explained what had happened, and with wonderful resilience they calmed down and eventually managed a shaky laugh or two. We went on our way with a little more care to the hand brake.

The Germany that I saw was a sad place. It was pitiful to see the defeated soldiers, in groups, or all alone, shuffling past, tramping home, journeying perhaps hundreds of miles, their uniforms in tatters and their feet bound into big bundles with rags. And horses and carts - one had never imagined the victorious German armies sweeping across Europe might have horses and carts somewhere in the background. The soldiers who managed to get lifts in these carts were the fortunate ones.

And while the millions of German ex-service people were trying desperately to reach their homes, many of which would now be in the Russian Zone, hundreds of thousands of DPs were being moved westward towards their homes, from one DP camp to the next. What those wandering German soldiers did for food, I have no idea, but the logistics of feeding the masses of DPs on their westward trek, added to the armies already settled in Germany, must have been immense.

Francis and I continued our trips to and from the UNRRA camp, delivering our loads of men and women one small step nearer their homes. I also made token appearances in the Cypher Office, where I was more of a hindrance than a help. Then, one shift, the Officer of the Watch came over to me as I sat idly at an empty machine,

"I think the time has come for you to go to the MO again - No!" as I opened my mouth to protest, "you really must: you're too sick to go on like this. You're just skin and bone. I want you to go now because the new MO has come: you'll like her. She's Austrian and very nice - not at all the same thing as your old friend. I'll make an appointment for you to see her tomorrow morning."

So the next morning I went along to the MO. I was met by the Medical Orderly, who apparently knew I was coming. She whispered to me,

"She's very nice; don't worry. Not like that old cat! She's gone!" which cheered me up a good deal and in I went.

I need not have been nervous: this new MO was young and very kind. She spoke English very well, with only a slight, rather pretty accent, and she was so different!

"I hear you're having a baby!" she greeted me, "Isn't that lovely? Your husband must be so pleased."

So thoroughly had that other woman upset me that she had smirched the whole thing and killed any feeling of joy I might have had. Now I realised that it was true, that we were going to have a child. I began to think, "This is rather nice." Then came the realisation that I knew next to nothing about babies, and whoever could I ask? My mother had had no children, she was in fact my stepmother, and she too was an only child. I'd have a lot of learning to do.

The MO confirmed that I was indeed pregnant, and said that she thought I should leave the army as soon as it could be arranged, in view of my health. She told me I could be demobilized under Paragraph 11, which provided for the release of pregnant women, or I could be released as an Officer's Wife. I can't remember just what the difference was, but I imagined that being released as an officer's wife would be the more pleasant way to do it. So that was arranged.

As for the nausea, she assured me that it would probably go of its own accord, and, as far as I can remember, prescribed nothing at all to combat it. Meanwhile I was excused duties whenever I didn't feel well.

The next day Francis came over on one of his regular visits and heard all about my visit to the MO and my being excused duties.

"Splendid!" he said, "How about coming back with me for a few days?"

"I can't go away with you just like that," I protested, "I'd be absent without leave. That would be a fine thing!"

"Well, why not apply for permission to come back with me? You're not doing much good here, are you?"

"I don't know," I said, "I suppose I'd have to ask the Officer of the Watch."

"Right," he said, picking up his cap and stick from the table, "let's go."

We went over to the Cypher Office and he waited while I went in and asked the Officer of the Watch if she would come and speak to my husband outside.

The pair of them went into conference outside the Cypher Office door. The Officer of the Watch readily agreed that it would be a very good thing if I could go with him and be looked after for a few days, but she had, she said, no authority to give permission. That would have to come from the Senior Commander herself and she suggested that we should go to see her.

The Senior Commander of the ATS in 21 Army Group was in her office, and we went in. She was quite aghast: what, give permission for one of her girls to go to an unknown formation (all men) miles away. She had never heard anything like it.

Francis told her that I had applied to be demobbed as an Officer's Wife, and that I was so sick that "she's no use to you, and I should be very glad to have her company."

She turned on me a look bordering on dislike:

"But where would she sleep?" He just refrained from preening his moustache and said that he thought he could be relied upon to arrange that. Good gracious, she couldn't permit that sort of thing. She supposed I might be able to sleep with the VADs in Brunswick. Now, I thought, I've heard everything.   I don't want to be parked in some hospital miles away every night. I expected him to accept and make a courteous withdrawal, but not so.

"No," I heard him say to my Ma'am, "I'm afraid that wouldn't do at all." She looked as surprised as I felt:

"That is the extent of my powers," she told him, "for anything further I should have to get permission from Brussels!" Obviously that was the end of the penny stage; she thought so, at any rate, and so did I, but my surprising husband merely said,

"What a excellent idea, Ma'am."

She made a remarkable recovery, gave me an icy look which told me plainly it was as well that I was getting out soon, and said,

"Sergeant, you may wait outside." With which the door was shut on me, leaving me to sit on an outsize laundry basket and swing my legs for a good half hour. At the end of that time of waiting, when I felt that I was going to bear the marks of the wicker basket on my person for the rest of my life, the door opened, Francis murmured some charming words of thanks and farewell, closed the door, grabbed me and said,

"Come on, we're going home."

And that is how I came to spend a week in the picturesque town of Osterode in the Hartz Mountains, in the house of the Town Major, a British army officer. Knowing the ways of Town Majors, you may be sure it was the most opulent house in the town, with wide, shallow, marble steps up to the entrance, and brass balustrades holding thick crimson ropes to help you totter up. The sitting room was furnished with immense settees and armchairs with bear skins thrown over them . . . very feudal, very 'twilight of the gods'. There was also a wintergarten, a conservatory where we had breakfast among plants and ferns and ate to the music of a fountain.

Our bedroom was quite splendid; big windows gave a view up the pine-clad slopes of the hills. Our bed had a feather mattress; sleeping in it was like relaxing in a cloud, and the sheets were linen and heavily encrusted with lace and embroidery. The pillows were covered with crimson silk pillowcases, and over them, starched white linen covers, embroidered with cut-work, so that the crimson showed through. The bedroom led into a bathroom, every surface completely covered in black or white marble.

As well as the Town Major and ourselves, there was a very beautiful woman staying in the house; she was a Countess, but whether German or Belgian I don't know. Her blond hair, of the palest honey colour, was twisted into a great shining knot in the nape of her neck. She was beautiful and elegant and sophisticated and I felt shy of her. She and the Town Major must have been business associates for, going into the sitting room one morning a little too early for breakfast, I found them deep in conference, with piles of paper money on the settee between them. I excused myself and fled: later that morning the Countess left for Brussels, and I never saw her again.

The complete rest in the Hartz Mountains did me good; I had nothing at all to do, but read, and that itself was a treat. Francis went off to work after breakfast, returning for lunch, and at least once I dined in his Mess. Everybody there was talking about getting out of the army. Now the fighting was over and the Zones of Occupation sorted out, it was the thought of civilian life that had become important, and at the back of their minds was the memory of what had happened at the end of the 1914-1918 war, when men were released from the forces and returned home with no jobs and no training except as soldiers. Again I began to wonder what Francis would do when he was released, but for some reason we didn't discuss it; it never occurred to me to ask him.

I went back to Bad Oeynhausen and reported in to the Office. I found that my application for release was being processed, and that all I had to do was to wait quietly and everything would come out right. In the meantime, a general election occurred and, for the first time in my life I voted. Much to my annoyance, Mr Churchill's government was not returned.

Francis was by now a firm favourite with our Mess staff and not only with the staff. Noticing that I couldn't face army margarine after American butter, he began bringing with him farm butter from Osterode, pale, almost colourless butter with little salt in it. To my disgust, I couldn't eat that either, but the rest of the Mess were very willing to eat it for me.

My release came through. A week or so before it arrived, a notice was circulated saying that all personnel returning to England were to be transferred by ship, not by plane, for economy, I suppose. My MO, however, would have none of it. She said that I was to fly, and she had her way.

Francis came over, a short, quick visit, and we said goodbye. I packed my kit for the last time and had my last meal in the Mess. As I was leaving one of the Orderlies who looked after us asked me to come into the kitchen, where the cook and the rest of the orderlies were waiting. I wondered whatever was going on.

With a sweet little speech the cook presented me with an outsize white loaf, absolutely stuffed with dried fruit. It was enormous, a jumbo loaf. It was the kindest gesture and I was very touched. We said goodbyes all round, and I thanked them for making Francis so welcome in the Mess, extra work for them, and then the truck arrived and I had to go.

I got in with all my equipment and baggage - even my little pillow - and we drove in silence to the airfield. I felt very sad, leaving the girls with whom I had worked and played for so long, and what lay ahead I simply could not envisage. But the main and immediate anxiety was, whatever to do with this elephant of a loaf, specially baked for me and innocent of any wrapping at all. There was no room for it in my kit, that was certain. I dithered: we were approaching the airfield. What, short of leaving it behind, was I to do with it? Just in time I wrapped it up in my greatcoat: I didn't need that in these warm summer days.

The aircraft was once again a DC3 troop carrier. As once before, I was the only person of such lowly rank, and all the rest were high-ranking officers of the Navy and Army. It was a bumpy flight and not at all what I should have liked. The pilot came back and announced that in view of the weather we would have to go up to 8,000 feet, and that it would be cold; he therefore advised all gentlemen (he can't have seen me) to put on their greatcoats.

There was a great putting-on of assorted greatcoats; I sat there mum-chance. Better be cold, than to expose that monster loaf in all its naked glory. But there was no escape: My neighbour on the bench was an Admiral, no less, and a courteous man. Seeing that I made no move to unfold my greatcoat and put it on, he stood up and before I could stop him, took it from my lap.

"My dear," he said, "let me help you. You mustn't get cold." Before I could stop him, he took my coat, gave it a vigorous shake and out flew my poor loaf, hit the deck and disintegrated into a million fruity crumbs all the length of the plane.

"Oh, my God, what have I done?" he said. I burst out laughing.

"My farewell present from the Mess cook! It wouldn't go in anywhere in my baggage. I couldn't think what to do with it."

The rest of the flight we spent chatting very pleasantly.

Croydon airport in the early morning, and a Sunday morning too, was quiet, but there was a truck to meet me which drove me to Chelsea Barracks, the demobilization centre. I had not even wondered how one got demobbed and I certainly never expected anything like this.

My driver ushered me into a vast room - it looked about an acre - and over it were spaced desks with soldiers sitting at them; I can't remember how many, I couldn't have counted them, anyway. Now I was ushered from table to table to be processed, rather like cheese. At every table I took one more step towards release from the army and return to civilian life. I signed forms, received a ration book, travel warrant, money, clothing coupons; I surrendered respirator, tin hat, mess kit, one uniform and that still crumby greatcoat. I kept all my more personal clothing, including my three pairs of blue and white striped pyjamas.

At the first table the NCO asked, "Where's the rest of the draft?" I said that as far as I could see, I was the draft. After that my demobbing became a really light-hearted affair, with everybody joining in the fun and I left to a chorus of 'goodbyes' and 'good lucks' and a lot of waving hands.

On this Sunday, 1st September 1945, I came out of the barracks feeling very odd - isolated, cut off, rather scared. I was on my own, free to do whatever I wanted to do, to go where I pleased; nobody to say yes, you may, or no, you may not. Unbelievably, I was bereft.

A taxi came along the road towards me: I raised my hand, and it slowed and stopped. The cabbie reached a hand back and opened the door. I climbed in with my remaining baggage.

"Where to, Sarge?"

Where to, indeed? For a moment I dithered. For three years the army had made my decisions for me, had fed me, clothed me, housed me, scolded me, sent me here and there

without asking my permission. Now I was out of the army
and I must make my own decisions.

I needed peace and quiet for a while, to get myself
sorted out, re-adjusted to civilian life. I needed to go home.

"Carshalton Beeches." I said.

CHAPTER 15

HOME

Oh, the utter relief of getting home. Out of the army, suddenly outside the system which, for the past three years, had taken over my life so completely, was an experience for which I was completely unprepared, and when Mother opened the door I felt a great rush of thankfulness.

She looked tired, I thought, but after all, was that surprising? Life had been pretty stressful for both her and my father for the last six years, six years of stress, shortages and fear, living on what was called Bomb Alley, the straight flight path the German bombers took to London. For months they had lived more in the shelter under the lawn than in the house, never knowing whether the house would be still there when they came out. Mother had been putting out incendiary bombs, doing emergency child-birth, never knowing from one day to the next if the rest of the family were alive or dead. It would take time to get over that.

We hugged each other, then I went up the stairs and dumped my baggage in my bedroom. It was good to be in it again, and I looked round it with affection, the yellow daisy covered walls, the white paint, the desk my father built for me to fit in to the corner, the little orange clock ticking away, the tulle curtains blowing in the breeze, the deep orange velvet ones that shut out the sun on those long summer evenings when I was still at school. Nothing had changed. I threw my cap on the bed and sat down, running my fingers through my hair. I was home again: I was safe in my nest.

Mother called up to me,

"Come and have a cup of tea." I went down and joined her in the kitchen. She poured out the tea, handed me a cup;

"There aren't any biscuits - I've got no more points left. Have you got a ration book?" I handed it over to her.

Her next words absolutely stunned me.

"How long are you thinking of staying?"

"Staying, Mummie? What do you mean? I've come home."

"My dear, this isn't your home any more. You're married now, and you're Francis's responsibility."

"But, Mummie, Francis is with his regiment - you know he is; what can he do?"

"Then you'll have to do something: you won't be able to stay here. There won't be enough room."

"But, Mummie, why not? I've got my own room; that's all I need."

"In a fortnight's time my mother will be coming to live here - she can't live alone any longer. She's ill."

"So am I!" I was practically weeping. "Where can I go? What can I do? What does Daddy say?"

"He agrees with me. You will have to find a place of your own."

"Mummie, you're not serious? You can't be! Everywhere's bombed flat, thousands of people are looking for homes, and you want me to walk out and find a house, just like that? I can't. I can't go anywhere far from home: I'm sick all the time."

"I'm afraid, dear, there's no more to be said. I can't tell you how sorry I am, but there it is."

"But if she's coming to live with you, can't I have her house? If I can't stay here in my own home, can't I rent it from her?"

"No, it's up for sale."

I got up heavily, left my tea, went back up the stairs on leaden feet, back into my room, my haven, my little nest, my shelter from the strange cold world outside. I shut the door and sat on the bed, then I dropped down on it, curled up and wept and wept.

Daddy was home by six. I heard him come in, and a little later he knocked at my door and came in. He sat on the bed by me, stroked the hair from my hot, wet face;

"Poor little love," he said, "I am so terribly sorry, and it's happened just when you need us most. Mummie's mother is suffering from dementia - she's no longer safe living alone. Goodness knows what's in store for your mother and me, and just when the war's over and we were looking forward to a rest."

"I don't like her," I said, "I never have, and she doesn't like me, and now she's pushing me out of my very own home. I hate her!"

"Try thinking of me, for a change," he said, very gently, wiping away the tears that kept on falling, "this is the second time in my life that I've had in-laws dumped on me, and your mother's not as strong as she was before the war."

Dinner, my first meal back in civvy street, was quiet: none of us found much to say. How different it all was from how I'd imagined it!

The next two weeks I spent looking for somewhere to live. I scanned the newspapers, caught trains and buses, walked untold miles, fighting the ever-present nausea that made any trip a hazardous adventure. I arrived last at the back of countless queues, all waiting for a chance of a house, a flat, even a room. Daily I dragged myself home, tired and sick and dispirited. I don't know what Mummie did: I imagine she must have been trying to sort out her mother's house, ready for the sale, in itself an immense job.

Looking back at that time, I can appreciate now the fix that both she and my father were in, and, as he said, at the end of all those years of bombing, danger, and shortages.

She was incredibly loyal and never mentioned that her mother's illness was a form of dementia which would only end with her death. This was just the beginning of a period of ever increasing care and watchfulness, and of incredible stress for both my father and for Mummie who nursed her mother for three long years until she died in 1948. My mother's health never recovered from the strain.

With time running out to find some sort, any sort of home, I was in despair: it was all too much, too futile. I hadn't the strength to go on, I couldn't go on. But where could I go, somewhere quiet and peaceful where I could rest and get myself better? In Hastings, Grandfather, now ninety, had sold my beloved Number 68, and was in an Eventide Home, and, from what I heard, the life and soul of the party. He couldn't help me.

My only hope was Grandfather's dear old friend, Uncle Fennell, who had been part of my life since I was small. A fruit importer, now retired, his big house in Silverhill had been my second home during school holidays when I stayed with my grandparents.

His housekeeper, Mammie King, had been a wonderful friend to me, a sort of no-nonsense combined stand-in mother and elder sister. Perhaps Uncle Fennell could put me up while I searched Hastings for somewhere to live. Things couldn't be as bad down there as they were up here. I rang her up.

"Mammie dear, would you have a scrap of room for me if I came down for a few days? I'm out of the army, and I've got to find somewhere to live. It's simply hopeless up here."

"Why aren't you staying with your people, love?"

"Mummie's mother is coming to live with them permanently, because she's ill, and Mummie says there won't be room for me. I don't really understand why."

"You'd better come on down. We've a Pay Corps captain billeted on us, but you can have the little bedroom over the porch. I'll tell your uncle you're coming."

It was as simple as that. I changed my uniform for civvies, packed a bag with clothes I'd had before I went into the army, said goodbye, and took a train down to Hastings.

CHAPTER 16

HAVEN

If Mammie King was surprised at my prompt appearance in Silverhill, she gave no sign.

"Well, this is nice! So you're out of the army, after all your adventures! Go and put your things in your room - you know which one. And then come down and we'll have a cup of tea, and you can tell me all about it."

"How are you, Mammie dear, and how are the kids?"

"Kids! Vickie's seventeen and has got herself a job in town: she's very much the young lady now. And John's almost eleven, and doing quite well at school. He reminds me more and more of his father. Ah, well . . . Go and put your things upstairs."

It was a tiny room, but it was bliss to be in it. I dumped my heavy case, tidied my hair and went downstairs. The kitchen was a big room, one wall completely filled with a great dresser, the shelves full of plates and enormous serving dishes. Opposite it stood the range, all blacklead and shiny knobs, and very rarely used. All the cooking was done on the gas stove in a smaller room opening off it which also had the pantry and the sink.

Next to the range was a cupboard reaching right up to the ceiling. The doors were open, and I could see that it was jammed, crammed, with bottled fruit, shelf above shelf, right up to the ceiling, and I knew that there would be more in one of the bathroom cupboards. The annual job of fruit bottling was over.

Most of the floor space was taken up with a huge scrubbed wood table. Mammie King was sitting there, waiting for me; she pushed a cup of tea towards me, and leaned back.

"Now, let's hear all about it."

"There's not much to tell," I said, "I'm still just shattered. I've been so sick - the army wouldn't let me come home by ship; they flew me. I just wanted to get home and, well, vegetate a bit, and get strong. But Mummie told me that her mother is moving in with them almost straight away, and there won't be any room for me. She's suffering from dementia, and can't be left on her own at all. I said I only needed my small room, but that didn't make any difference. I've been trying everywhere to find somewhere to live, Mammie, I really have, but it's hopeless - everybody's looking for somewhere to live, and it's awful going all over the place house-hunting, in buses and trains, and you're always too late, and all the time you don't know if you're going to be sick." My voice began to wobble and I stopped.

"I reckon your mother's going to have her hands full, my dear. She's probably desperate about it all. It's no joke looking after somebody with that sort of illness, and it gets worse as time goes on. If you hadn't been having your baby she mightn't have felt so trapped, but the two together, well, I think she felt she simply couldn't manage."

"What am I to do, Mammie? You've got a houseful yourself. There's Uncle, and you, and Vickie and John, and your billeted officer and now me. I can't stay here very long."

She didn't look too bothered:

"Have you brought your ration book?" I handed it over. "Oh, a green one! Of course! This is for you and the baby. With a bit of luck you may get an orange or a banana now and then."

She rose, went over to the dresser and put it in a vast tureen to join a small pile of brown ration books. She came back and sat down.

"Now, stop worrying. You'll stay here just as long as you need to. You've much more chance of finding something here than you have nearer London. Just relax and take it quietly. And now I think you should go and say 'Hello' to Uncle. He's been looking forward to your coming. He's in the dining room."

Uncle was always in the dining room; his red velvet winged chair stood by the fire, and next to the chair, on a table against the wall, stood his radio. Nobody could possibly call it a wireless - there were wires everywhere and knobs galore and the loud speaker was an elegant brown horn. I'd never seen a radio like it anywhere else. Years ago, when I was a kid at school, Uncle and I had sat here, he in the red velvet chair, and I on a footstool, and listened to the Schneider Trophy races. The races were flown over the Solent by sea planes and the winner was a plane called a Supermarine Spitfire that had a Rolls Royce engine. It became the prototype of the famous Spitfire fighter planes.

Uncle was a tall man, gentle and courteous, still handsome, and with wonderful white curly hair; he dressed elegantly in the fashion of his youth, with narrow trousers, and wing collars. As I opened the door I saw him; he was lying back in his red velvet chair; his eyes were closed and the radio was playing music very softly; I wondered if was from Radio Luxemburg which had always been the best station for Hastings. He didn't hear me come in, and for a moment I stood looking round the room.

Nothing had changed; the velvet sofa stood in the bay window, a small fire burned in the grate, the flames reflected in points of light from brass andirons, polished till they looked like gold. Over the fire stood the elaborate overmantel, with mirrors and lots of twisted little columns holding up small shelves of photographs.

Against the wall stood the huge sideboard, ten or twelve feet long, loaded with silver, tea services, a stand with egg cups and spoons, cruets and numerous shooting trophies Uncle had won.

Curled in the niche between the sideboard's two pedestal cupboards lay Uncle's great brindled dog, Bruce, half asleep. He opened one eye at me, thumped his tail a few times and dozed off again. He must be very old - he'd been around ever since I could remember. His father was a Great Dane and his mother, a Mastiff, had been wounded on active service in the First World War, before I was born, carrying despatches along the trenches.

Strictly speaking Bruce was not a house dog. He was only allowed in the dining room if he lay in the space between the sideboard cupboards, because of the disaster he caused one sad day: a family celebratory meal was about to take place and all was ready, the table set with silver and the Crown Derby china. Bruce, very excited, ran around the room, and his great tail swept just about every single thing off the table. That was a considerable smash.

Uncle opened his eyes and saw me. As I came across the room towards him he stood up. He put his hands on my shoulders and kissed me.

"It's good to see you, my dear. Mrs King tells me you've not been very well. You're very thin - you've lost a lot of weight! Sit down, sit down. You must tell us how we can help. You're not to rush into anything, you know; just go gently, and remember, we want you to stay with us until you're properly fixed up with somewhere to live."

We sat and smiled at each other, and the room was quiet, the fire made soft noises to itself, and a little blue flame appeared from under a coal, and waved like a small flag. I lay back watching it and felt the strain and misery of these last two weeks slipping gently away. All would be well.

That afternoon I met Captain Stanley who was billeted on Uncle. He had been wounded in North Africa and, unfit to return to his regiment, he had been seconded to the Pay Corps, where he would have to stay until he was demobbed.

Then Vickie, Mammie King's daughter, and eight years younger than I, came home, grown up and very pretty, and John came home from school. The family was complete. I relaxed. I was safe; I wasn't homeless any more.

*   *   *

Life fell into a quiet routine. Uncle looked after his flowers, his peach and nectarine houses, the budgerigars in their big cage, and the vegetable garden, and in the late afternoon I accompanied him on walks to listen to the nightingales in the woods near Shornden reservoir. We stood silently, Uncle leaning on his stick, his handsome head tilted, listening to the incredible song rising and falling, rising and falling, sheer liquid beauty. And at last Uncle would rouse himself: "A sweetly pretty song, my dear, the most beautiful song in the world. They love to be near water." And we continued on.

Every morning, directly after breakfast, Captain Stanley disappeared and was away till dinner time. Vickie went to her job, John to school, and when the dust of their departure had died down, Mammie and I whipped round the house and restored it to some degree of tidiness. She wasn't a committed housewife like my mother, but the place always looked good. Often I did the family shopping for her. The constant nausea which had plagued me for months was passing and I began to enjoy these expeditions. Now and again when I went shopping I was presented with a banana or an orange, just as Mammie had predicted, a tremendous treat, and one which only holders of green ration cards were likely to receive.

The weeks slipped past, and we entered October. The leaves were turning to their wonderful autumnal tints and the days, crisp and cool and still sunny, were drawing in. I felt better and better. It was good to be alive.

This morning I set out for town with Mammie King's shopping list. I would have to catch the trolley bus at the top of the hill, and go right down into Hastings. I walked smartly up the hill till I reached the bus stop, just outside a newsagent's shop. While I stood waiting I passed the time looking at the newsagent's window. In these days, after all the years of war and shortages, there wasn't much in it, a few books with sun-curled pages, and what I strongly suspected were cardboard models of bars of chocolate. Outside, nailed to the wall, was a noticeboard, covered with a protective grille. There were a few notices, and I read them. 'For sale,' said one, 'Blue budgerigar. To good home only.' 'For sale, carpet square, 10' X 10' autumn leaves, slightly worn. £5.' I didn't want a budgie, and I had nowhere to put a carpet. I turned my back on the shop to look up the road for the bus.

At that moment, the newsagent came out of the shop, a postcard in his hand. He opened the grille, pinned the postcard on the board, closed the grille, and went back inside.

Idly, I read the notice. 'To let. Unfurnished flat, living room, bedroom, kitchen, bathroom, big garden. Apply 27 Magdalen Road.'

Magdalen Road! There was a church there and a little school! That was the school I had gone to for a whole year after my mother died; I was five and living with my grandparents. One beautiful autumn, just like this one, I used to walk there from Number 68, shuffling ankle-deep through crisp, gorgeous coloured leaves.

With which the trolley bus drew up beside me. I swung up and on board. "Magdalen Road, please." I said.

Minutes later I found myself knocking at the door of 27 Magdalen Road. One of a long terrace of houses with bay windows and tall, pillared porches, it reminded me very much of dear Number 68, on the next hill. The door was opened by a woman a bit older than I, and very pregnant.

"I've come about the flat," I said hesitantly, "Has it gone?"

"No, it hasn't," she said, "Where did you see the notice?"

"I was waiting for a bus at Silverhill," I said, "The newsagent came out and put it up right in front of me."

"I only gave it to him a quarter of an hour ago! Come and see the flat."

It was the basement flat. As we went down the steps she told me that before she married her name was Freebody; her father had been a partner in the London firm, Debenham and Freebody, and this had been the family home. Now that her parents were dead, she and her husband had found the house far too big, and they had divided it into three flats. They had the road level one, and an elderly couple had the one above that. They had just got the bottom flat ready to let. She opened the green front door and ushered me in.

At the front there was a big sitting room; it was below the level of the road, but the steps down and the area outside had been painted a warm cream and the room itself was newly decorated with cream walls, and looked full of sunshine. Behind it was a smaller room, the bedroom, looking over the garden. Between the two rooms there was a small windowless room, a store room, I supposed, and then, at the end of the long passage, the kitchen, also newly painted. A door led out to a paved area and then to a long garden which sloped downhill. It was very neglected, but I saw that it was full of fruit trees, still bearing apples and pears and some plums. At the bottom of the garden a gate opened on to a narrow right of way which led to the road. I had been wondering however I could get a pram up and down those area steps. Now I realised I would never need to do that. I could come in through the garden gate and push the pram straight up the path and into the kitchen.

There was a loo, I discovered, in exactly the same position as in Number 68, outside the kitchen door.

"Where's the bathroom?"

"That's the snag. There's only one, to serve the three flats, and it's up three flights of stairs, at the top of the house."

"Oh." I said. That certainly was a snag.

"Look," she said, " If you like the place, I'll tell you what I'll do. I'll have a hand basin put into the bedroom. It would only have cold water, but it'll be better than nothing. What do you think"

Nothing in life is perfect. It was a roof.

"I'd like to take it," I said, "What does one do? Should I give you some rent in advance?" She patted my arm;

"Don't bother about it now. I haven't got a rent book anyway - I'll have to go and get one. Come around tomorrow morning and we'll settle it all up."

A horrible thought struck me:

"I can't move in yet. I'm only just out of the army, and I haven't got any furniture. It'll take me a time to get organised."

"Same here. I was in the WAAF. What were you in?"

"ATS. Look, I forgot to tell you I'm having a baby. Do you mind? Some people do."

She patted her tummy.

"Look at me!"

CHAPTER 17

SIDI DAUD

I practically danced my way back up the road and it was by sheer chance that I remembered to do Mammie King's shopping for her. Back at Uncle's I marched into the kitchen, where Mammie was finishing a pile of ironing and dumped the shopping on the table.

Mammie stood the iron up on its heel:

"Where've you been all this time? I thought you'd got lost." I swung the key on my finger;

"Look, Mammie! Look what I've got! I've found a flat!"

"Never! Where?"

"Magdalen Road."

"How did you find it?"

"Let's have a cup of tea and I'll tell you all about it. Goodness, I feel quite tired!"

Mammie King was just about as excited as I was.

"What an amazing bit of luck! I told you you'd have more chance down here, but I never dreamed it would happen so quickly. Shall we go and see it after lunch?"

Now more bits of luck came my way. It was as if the little god of luck was making amends for the unhappiness of my first weeks out of the army. Vickie had a friend who had just got married and not only had she received her entitlement of the coupons necessary to buy furniture, but her enormous family had done her really well, and had given her furniture from their own homes, so that she had a beautifully appointed home and had not even used her coupons. These she gave to me, so that with my own allowance of coupons and hers I was really well off.

I rang my parents and told them the good news: they were delighted and told me they would have a bedroom suite brought down to me by Carter Paterson; they'd arrange it straight away. The suite was oak; my own mother had bought it when she was first married, during the Great War, so it was old fashioned, but what did that matter? They would also send me bed linen and pillows, some rugs they didn't need and there were some tea things and dinner plates and a saucepan or two.

The next excitement was that Francis got some leave, and we went shopping together for dining room furniture. Furniture making, as with the production of china and pottery, was strictly controlled by Government. Nothing fussy was permitted. All dining room suites had to be made to a pattern, called Utility, in which the timber could be cut to the very best advantage. The names of the makers were not permitted to appear, so you could be lucky and buy pieces which had been made by craftsmen, and equally you could be unlucky, and buy pieces that were just the opposite. The girl who gave me the coupons had somehow discovered how to identify the makers by their private marks; she showed me, and that was very useful.

Francis and I came home that day having bought a dining room suite comprising a square extending table, four chairs and a sideboard. There were enough coupons to allow us to buy a square occasional table and a utility radio to stand on it. We also bought a Canon gas stove and an Ascot water heater which we arranged to be installed over the kitchen sink.

That was it. Our home was furnished, more or less. Francis was charmed with it. He said it reminded him of a dug-out which was his home in Tobruk, in an area called Sidi Daud, at the 60-pounder gun battery they had inherited from the Australians. He called the flat Sidi Daud ever after.

After he had gone back to Germany, I was ready to move in, but then I had a set-back: I woke up full of energy, got out of bed, put on my dressing gown and started out to the bath room. On the way I met John, going in the same direction. Like an idiot, I decided to race him. Just as I reached the bathroom door, with my hand already on the door frame, he pushed ahead of me and slammed the door, catching the top joint of my right hand ring finger and crushing it. I felt one moment of dreadful pain and then - nothing.

"John," I called, "Do open the door: you've got my finger in the door."

"Funny story," he called back, "I've won. You'll have to wait."

"Please, John! I can't get my finger out."

After a bit more pleading, he opened the door and I took my finger out. It was white and dead, and split down both sides and all round the nail. It didn't hurt. John went back into the bathroom and was sick. I went downstairs, where Mammie King and Captain Stanley were breakfasting.

"I've hurt my finger." I said. Captain Stanley took my hand, and looked at it.

"Oh, dear, that's nasty."

"It doesn't hurt." I said.

"It will."

He fetched the First Aid box and dressed it. I felt rather sick myself.

"Come," said Mammie, "It's warm in the dining room. You can lie down on the sofa for a little while. That's going to hurt when it comes to life again." It did. Like hell.

When everybody had gone their various ways, Mammie King came in to me.

"Well, you're going to need a doctor anyway, for the baby. So we'd better go and see what Dr Howe says about that finger. He's Uncle's doctor; he's getting on a bit, but all the young doctors are still away in the forces. Can you dress by yourself?"

Doctor Howe seemed pleased with the baby; nothing to worry about there, he said. All was going very nicely and he'd see me next month. But he shook his head over the crushed finger on my right hand; I'd lose the nail, he said, and he rather doubted whether another one would grow. It would depend on the damage to the nail bed. Perhaps, as I was pregnant, it might grow back. He strapped it up professionally and then Mammie and I walked back home and had a soothing cup of tea.

I'm left handed and I had never realised how much I used my right hand. This was going to be a tedious, long drawn out business and a real handicap. Mammie decided I'd better wait a week or two before moving into the flat. There'd be such a lot of work to do and I'd need both hands.

Sore hand or not, I spent several days at Sidi Daud, on my knees sanding the bare floor boards in the sitting room, staining them with permanganate of potash, and then polishing them. The bedroom suite and other things arrived from home, and the firm delivered the new furniture. The floors were a bit patchy, but they didn't look bad with the rugs from home spread on the boards.

On my birthday, exactly one year since I landed in Normandy, I moved into Sidi Daud. I laid the week's rations out in the big empty pantry, where they made an unimpressive sight, a little sugar and tea, two ounces of butter - or was it three? Four ounces of margarine, four ounces of cheese and so on.

I put my night things on the bed, under the pillows, and looked at my watch. Half past twelve already! No wonder I was hungry: I needed some lunch.

It was only then that the horrid truth dawned on me. If I wanted to eat, I'd have to make the food myself, not only now, but in the far foreseeable future, too. And all I had ever done in the way of food preparation was to make cucumber sandwiches for tea and to cook bacon and eggs twice for Francis, which wasn't much help, with one egg a week on my ration card.

In those first few weeks in the flat I learned a lot about the basics of housekeeping. Mammie King was marvellous: she would arrive with a basket-full of bits and pieces, a bottle of plums, or a thick slice of fruit cake, even a cut off their big roasted joint, and how I did appreciate these gifts from heaven!

I learned something else, too, and it was about myself. Not for years had I been alone, actually physically alone, with nobody around. I wasn't prepared for the solitude, and the silence of the little flat made me uneasy. I began to turn the radio on when I got up in the morning, and to leave it on when I went out shopping: it was so comforting and friendly to hear a voice talking when I opened the front door.

Grandfather, established in the Eventide Home on the next hill, walked over occasionally and had tea with me, and the girl upstairs would wander down for a chat, though after her baby was born she didn't have much time and I saw less of her.

By now I was six months pregnant, it was November, and the lovely autumn had turned into cold, wet winter, with bitter south-westerly gales blowing up the Channel. Even with the fire burning in the sitting room it was cold, and it was an act of determination to leave the fire and go to the outside loo. I came home from shopping one day, picking up the mail from the mat. There was a letter from Francis.

I set down my basket and the letters on the kitchen table, and unlatched the back door to go to the loo. As I opened the door, the gale snatched it out of my hands; it crashed back and a spray of icy rain wet me from head to foot. I struggled to shut the door, then made my way miserably to the loo. Coming back, wet and frozen, I had to lean with all my strength against the door to force it shut.

I sat down at the table, and opened Francis's letter. Water from my hair dripped on it. A photograph fell out: it was Francis, on skis and laughing. The letter said he was on leave in the Hartz Mountains, having a great time, lovely sunny weather, and he was getting quite brown. I dropped the letter on the table, put my head on it and wept.

Francis got forty-eight hours leave for Christmas. It was wonderful. I made some inexperienced sort of Christmas cake and I think I decorated it with some sort of fruit jellies, since I had nothing else. Anyway he was complimentary, whatever it cost him. I also decided that for his first meal I must impress him with how much I had learned about cooking. I was rather short of fats, but I had plenty of apples. I'd make an apple pie. I'd not tried pastry before, but I'd seen Grandma make it lots of times, though for some reason she'd never let me take over, though I was sure I could. I made the pie, and that lunch time brought it to the table.

Francis was duly impressed: he uttered the classic "By Jove! Apple pie! Just like mother used to make!" and pressed his fork into the crust.

There was a loud crack, the crust broke into bits, and a large piece flew right across the room and hit the wall. Francis burst out laughing and I burst into tears. Such are the trials of a learner cook on rations!

He left for Germany directly after Christmas, and my life settled down again, but in January, when I was eight months pregnant, I had a most surprising letter from him. His colonel, his major and he were all coming over to do a course on three-quarter tracked vehicles at the Royal Artillery School of Mechanical Traction at Rhyll. It was a week's course, and as they were to stay in an hotel, wives were invited. Did I want to come? Did I!

He arrived one evening, helped me pack and we started off the next morning for London. It was very pleasant to be travelling with him, going First Class, with whatever comforts were available - life was getting a bit wearisome now. It would be good to stay in an hotel, with no work to do. The train left Warrior Square Station, I settled into my seat and opened my book, Francis opened a book with a khaki cover and immediately became immersed in it; the train rocked peacefully on its way over the flat pastures that border Pevensey Bay.

Without any warning there was a crash and the train stopped with a jerk that unshipped me from my seat. From under the train came the hiss of escaping air and then there was silence. I settled myself more comfortably and read on. I'd reached the thrilling part of my book.

"What was that?" asked Francis, sitting in the window seat opposite me, finger marking the place in his book.

"Cow on the line." I didn't bother to look up. He stood up, let down the window and leaned out, letting in a blast of cold air and the sound of voices from the front of the train.

"He drew back his head and looked at me: "How did you know?"

"Huh? Know what?"

"About the cows." he said. I got up, leaned out. Just opposite the window a man was standing on the track.

"Got yer ration book, Mum?" he called, and held up the amputated still-bleeding leg of a cow.

I sat down and felt ill. The train, unable to stop, had ploughed into a herd of dairy cattle crossing the line to another pasture in charge of a German prisoner of war.

The shoe which collected the electricity from the live rail was broken, and we sat there, helpless, waiting for a repair gang to bring spare parts.

"Are you feeling all right?" Francis looked anxious.

"I've just been thinking," I said, "I was in a jeep crash outside Heidelburg, when we were rammed by a drunken GI. I made a forced landing in a DC3 when somebody sabotaged it and it caught fire. And now this. That's road, air and rail. This baby was meant to be born. I wonder what he'll be."

"Probably go to sea!" said my husband.

The stay at Rhyll made a delightful change, even though Francis was busy all day, and had plenty to discuss with the others in the evening. At least we had the nights together. I rested, went for walks and one day took myself to the cinema where another Artillery Officer sat beside me and we chummed up. He showed me pictures of his wife and children, and we got on like a house on fire. It did quite something for my morale which in view of my rapidly increasing girth had taken a bit of a nose dive.

February. Colder and wetter and windier. I didn't go up to Uncle's any more; the weather was too bleak, but Mammie King kept an eye on me and it was so good to see her coming down the steps. I had been wondering quite a bit about the coming birth, and realised I knew nothing at all about it. Who could I ask? My stepmother had never had a child. I didn't like to ask the girl upstairs. No, I'd have to ask Mammie - she'd had two. She'd know all about it. At least I wasn't as ignorant as a girl I knew who had gone to have her baby expecting her tummy to pop open like a pea pod and the baby to pop out.

When I asked Mammie, she didn't answer at once. She thought about it a bit and then said that the best way of describing it was - that it was like a bad attack of constipation. With that I had to be content, though it left me as much in the dark as ever.

February Fill-Dyke! The month dragged on its weary way. Towards the end of the month the weather dried up a bit and turned colder still. On the Sunday I woke up feeling full of energy. I dressed, went to early Mass up the road, came back, and started to give the kitchen a real clean: it hadn't seemed too bad the day before. I worked all morning, and at lunch time, sat down at the dining room table and had some soup and a sandwich. As I stood up to take the plates back into the kitchen I suddenly felt wet and to my horror I saw a puddle on the floor. How absolutely disgusting. I went into the kitchen and a line of drips followed me. There was something here that I didn't understand. I suddenly felt the need for some reassurance. I went to my next door neighbour.

She was quite a bit older than I; her husband was a retired university lecturer and they had three grown-up children. When she came to the door, I said,

"Look. What's that?"

"Oh, my dear," she said, "You've started your baby. Is your bag packed?"

"Oh, yes, it's been ready for ages. But I don't feel anything." I thought of Mammie and her description of childbirth.

"Don't worry about that. Go and get your case and come back here. I'm ringing for a taxi."

I went and got my bag, and was soon being bowled along to the luxurious nursing home where I was booked in. They gave me a big room, with chintz covered armchairs and a view of the main road.

By evening things had changed. My back hurt and I couldn't sit or lie in comfort. I stood at the window, watching the traffic going up and down. It was growing dark and the street lights were on; they were mercury vapour ones, which turned everything to a nasty eerie green. The trolley buses were green, the pavements were green, the bare, wind-blasted trees were green. It began to snow, gently at first, and then harder, and the whirling flakes were green. The snow lay on the pavements, green on green. Never in all my life had I felt so miserable, so forsaken, so bereft of all those I loved. It was a long night.

Christopher was born at half past seven the next morning, and very soon afterwards Dr Howe puffed his way into my room. There was a lot of laughter, though I couldn't see anything funny. The nursing staff thought the baby looked so much like Francis that all he needed was a moustache. There was more laughter when they realised that the nursing home was so full of unexpected births that they had run out of cots. They took the bottom drawer from the chest of drawers in my room, put a pillow in it for a mattress and tucked him up. He didn't seem to mind.

CHAPTER 18

CHRISTOPHER

Whoever said that the birth of a child changes one's life was dead right. I had had quite enough to do looking after myself, and learning to cook and look after the tiny flat. I managed to look after Francis when he came home on his short trips, but this was ridiculous! This tiny scrap of humanity required looking after all the time! He needed feeding every four hours, he presented me with revolting nappies at short intervals, and when I just wanted to lie down and close my eyes and rest he roared with rage - or that's what I thought it must be.

Mother came down for a few days to help me over the first week or so. She must have employed a nurse for her mother. Perhaps it was a relief to get away, even though on arriving she took over the running of the household. It was lovely to have her. We made an expedition and bought a pram; it was black with a cream lining and high wheels, beautifully sprung. Now I could be properly mobile and go shopping with the baby, and have somewhere to put the things I bought and take him for walks. It was also while she was staying with me that we went exploring secondhand shops and I bought a two-seater settee for the astronomical sum of £30. It wasn't particularly beautiful, but it was something to relax on: apart from that I had only the four dining chairs.

Our baby was baptised at the church only a little way from Sidi Daud and named Christopher Godfrey, Christopher because that was what I had chosen while I was still in Germany, and Godfrey for Francis's father, who had died before Francis's eleventh birthday. Christopher's godmother was the lady who lived in the top flat of Number 27. Mammie King came, too, looking very elegant with an up-swept hair do.

Mother couldn't stay any longer: she went back home, and I did miss her. Mammie King came down when she could, but she was busy and the weather was awful. My great delight was to find a letter from Francis on the front door mat. His letters were full of interesting things. In fact, they became more and more interesting: he had made friends, he told me, with the German District Forest Officer in charge of the forests round Osterode, and with whom he dealt when he went into the forest to hunt for deer to feed their Mess and the troops. The deer had apparently multiplied during the war years to such an extent that they were damaging the forest.

A District Forest Officer's life seemed very attractive, he said, and a far cry from life in the little bank in Wallington, with the cosy clientèle and honey sold under the counter. He was thinking of going to university when he was demobbed, and studying for a degree in forestry. I wasn't sure what to say in reply, except that the bank did seem a bit small for a man who had lived his sort of life for more than six and a half years and who spent his spare time stalking deer.

His next letters took my breath away. He had been given a demobilization number, Age and Service Group 27. The Other Ranks Group 27 had already left the army and were settling back into civilian life. Officers would have to wait longer, but it wouldn't be long now.

I couldn't believe it! To have Francis home here with me, every day, not in the army any more! How wonderful! What would it be like? What was normal married life like, anyway? What was normal? It was too far away to remember.

The weather abated, and I began to take Christopher for walks in his pram, down to the front to look at the sea. I've always had a yen to live by the sea, in sight of the sea, and we spent quite a time there.

One sunny day, May the 16th, Francis came home. In a way it was funny, because, having been demobbed that morning, he was no longer an officer with men at his beck and call. He arrived by taxi, all the way from Aldershot, and I understood why very quickly: his baggage was enormous. There was a huge valise, several kit bags, and a great carved wooden chest, which the cabbie and he manoeuvred carefully down the steps, and that was followed by an odd shaped bundle, heavily swathed, which when unwrapped turned out to be a round oak table two feet across, which matched the oak chest. He paid off the cabbie, who departed in great good humour, and then we stood among the baggage and looked at each other.

"Well," he said, wrapping me in a bear hug, "that's that, and about time too. Now we can begin our proper lives."

I took him by the hand:

"Come and meet your son. It's disgraceful: he's three months old and you've never seen him."

Christopher was fast asleep in his cot by the bed. Francis leaned over and inspected him gingerly.

"Hmm, he looks pretty normal." he said, "Now . . ."

We had begun our proper lives.

* * *

Francis had spent the last weeks of his army career at Göttingen University, swotting up the subjects he would need if he managed to get into a university. Now I began to see the intense drive he directed into anything he was determined to do. He applied for admission to the four universities which offered courses in forestry and all four sent him their prospectuses.

Meantime, he was on full army pay for something like six months, which was a great help. But if he were to get into one of the universities he would have first to get some practical experience in the forests, so he'd better find himself a job as soon as possible. I didn't understand.

"What sort of a job?"

"Just as a labourer in the forest." He leaned back in his exquisite uniform, and regarded me, "What did you expect? They don't have special places for demobbed officers in the forest service."

He applied for a job with the Forestry Commission and was invited to come - with his wife - to be interviewed the following week at Woking.

"But we can't." I was appalled, "That's the day Mammie King is looking after Christopher and we're meeting Eileen and Leslie in London and going to see *Arsenic and Old Lace*. It's been fixed for ever!"

"No worries: we'll take an earlier train and do the interview on the way."

Francis has always maintained that when we went into the interview room, with its table full of men, Francis in his Service Dress uniform, and I in a grey worsted suit and the white chiffon blouse from my trousseau, to be interviewed for a job where he would be using billhook and sickle in the forest, they nearly dropped. Whatever they thought, he got the job.

We had a marvellous time that day in London, and then came back and collected Christopher from Mammie King. He seemed very pleased to see us and rewarded us with gummy smiles. That day was the last occasion for a long time when we could dress up and have an adult outing.

Francis started work and at first found it very hard going. Early every morning, dressed in battle dress and army boots, he went off on his bike, sent down from Carshalton. He returned in the evening, pretty tuckered out. He took his lunch with him, and I began to get up early, make his sandwiches and a hefty breakfast and wave him goodbye. Sidi Daud was at the top of a steep hill: Warrior Square Station was at the bottom. Francis said goodbye, got on his bike, sailed down the garden path, out of the gate, down the hill and straight on to the platform. As he grew more experienced, he discovered that his train left Hastings Station, plunged into the long tunnel which ran deep under our hill and out into Warrior Square Station. As it entered the tunnel it hooted: if Francis then kissed me goodbye, leapt on his bike and coasted off, he would arrive on the platform just as the train entered the station. He got so good at this that when one day he was delayed for a few minutes to pump up a soft tyre, the train obligingly waited for him.

It was great fun having Francis home.

Spring was well established: the fruit trees in the garden were decked with blossom, pink and white. The days were drawing out, and Christopher lay in his pram in the garden kicking chubby and surprisingly strong legs. By now Francis had settled well into his job in the forest and had developed hefty muscles. The nappies no longer bothered me: they danced and snapped on the line and dried in no time at all. We acquired a little 'granite' cat, a grey and white tabby, and Francis named her Binti, which he told me was Arabic for girl. Binti was lost for a whole day before her muffled cries led us at last to Francis's clothes cupboard where we discovered her head first down one of his tall army boots, the sort that were boots and leather gaiters combined.

Francis received a summons to Oxford, to be interviewed by Professor Champion. He went to Oxford for the interview, and came back saying that he'd learnt a lot, and that it was, of course, a wonderful place, but he really couldn't bear the prospect of living in the Thames valley, dank and cold in winter and hot and steamy in the summer. Also, he doubted very much whether he'd be able to find anywhere for us to live. The place appeared to be bursting at the seams. He rather preferred the sound of Aberdeen.

He went for his interview in Aberdeen by the night train and walked out into the sparkling summer morning of the granite city. He was enchanted. At the university he was interviewed by the Professor of Forestry, Prof Steven, who asked him what links his family had with Scotland. He thought for a moment and then said that his wife was a Grant, a clan well established in the North East of Scotland. The Prof gave a small smile, and sent him to the Aberdeen Conservator of Forests for a recommendation that he was 'a suitable person to be trained as a Forest Officer.'

Interviews over, Francis returned home and resumed his job as a forest worker. A few weeks later he was notified that he had been accepted by both Balliol and Aberdeen. At Aberdeen he was offered one of twenty places. There were four hundred applicants.

Straight away he accepted Aberdeen's offer. We had a real celebration, and when we had our feet on the ground again he said he thought the time had come to give up his job in the forests: he must go up to Aberdeen and try to find somewhere for us to live.

Christopher and I saw him off at the station and then I pushed the pram up that steep, steep hill back to Sidi Daud. The place felt very empty, and so did I. My family had lived in Sussex for hundreds of years and I didn't want to go to what amounted to a foreign country; this was my own, my native land. I made the best of the lovely weather and Christopher and I went for miles every day. We went up to see Mammie King, and told her what was happening, we went round the garden with Uncle and admired the peach houses, festooned now with the nets which would catch any fruit that fell. We went down our hill and up the next one to see Grandpa, and Grandpa was charmed with his only great-grand child. Mummie made a brief visit - things were getting pretty bad at home; she looked tired and couldn't stay. She took a photograph of me, with

Grandpa holding Christopher, and she managed to set her camera and run back in time to be included in the photograph, so that four generations were together in the picture.

A letter came from Francis; he sounded tired and dispirited. He was combing the countryside for accommodation and having no luck at all. It was the same old story: I knew it so well, and my heart bled for him. Having no transport of his own, he had to rely on trains and buses and his own two feet to go to any place offered for rent, and like me, he inevitably arrived at the back of the crowd. Poor Francis.

But I had already seen a glimpse of that steely determination which he had developed during his years in the army. When he set his mind on something he spared no effort at all to get what he wanted; and eventually he found something. By this time his search in ever increasing circles from Aberdeen had brought him to the little hill village of Torphins, and there he found Mrs Anderson, a woman with a heart of gold. She couldn't give us a flat of our own, she said, but we could have a living room and a bedroom and use of her kitchen - and, of course, of the bathroom. He accepted joyfully and caught the next train home.

In September, with the summer slipping away, we made our goodbyes, and oh, they were difficult. We said goodbye to Mammie King and Uncle and Vickie and John - who was delighted to find that my finger nail had grown again perfectly; we visited Grandpa and said goodbye to him. He was now in his nineties, still full of fun and walking very well; we said goodbye to our WAAF landlady upstairs. The removal men who were on their way back to Scotland put our small possessions in their van and disappeared, and we - we caught the train for London and, after spending the night with my parents, we took the express train to Aberdeen to arrive in time for breakfast at the station restaurant - porridge and kippers, butteries and marmalade.

Aberdeen University

CHAPTER 19

TORPHINS

It was September when I first saw Torphins, and the hills around the village were bright with heather. I saw a small village of granite houses set down in miles of farm land. There were a few shops, a chemist who was also the postmaster and had a library - about three feet by six feet, a school, two churches and a very large hotel, the Learney Arms, called after Sir Thomas Innes of Learney, the Laird, the local land owner. Not only was he the Laird: he was Lord Lion King of Arms, the ultimate authority on all matters of heraldry in Scotland and an important figure at all functions connected with the Royal Family when they took their annual holiday at Balmoral.

Mrs Anderson's house was one of the few houses on Auchmacoy Road, which began at the station and ended miles away in a tiny village called Tornaveen. Her house was on the right, and next to it was the Cottage Hospital with the village's little War Memorial outside on the road. Opposite Mrs Anderson's was the North of Scotland Bank, the ground floor room of a private house - the bank manager lived in the rest - and the next building was the tiny police station where Sandy the Policeman lived with his wife, Maidie. One room of the cottage was his office, and in the garden there were two cells for evil-doers. Later on I discovered that there never were any evil-doers - apart, from that is, the occasional man caught poaching salmon, which, from the village's point of view, was hardly a crime, just a bit of carelessness in being caught.

There was a way of 'guddling' them, very gently putting your hand into the water and waiting till a fish swam over to inspect, waiting till your hand was under him, and then gently tickling his tummy. He would hang in the water quite still, entranced, until with a sudden quick scoop, you swept him up, out of the water and on to the bank. I can't remember anyone being charged with guddling salmon; a quiet word from Sandy was all it took. The cells in the garden remained empty of evil-doers, and one was furnished with bed, dressing table and wardrobe for when Maidie's mother came to stay. The other cell was used as accommodation for the odd back-packer who turned up in the village, short of money and lodgings.

Mrs Anderson's front door opened straight on to the pavement, though I don't remember anyone ever using the front door. Everybody automatically went round to the back and came in through the kitchen. We did, too, that first day, and Francis introduced me to her. She was a large, plump, motherly woman, and made me very welcome. She showed me the room that was to be our bedroom, and the front room that we were to use as a living room. Our furniture had not arrived yet, but when it did, there was plenty of room to put it in the shed in the garden. It would be quite all right there - it was nice and dry; it had been her husband's workshop.

I can't say I was happy straight away with my new way of life. I was so far away from my parents, from Grandpa, from Mammie King and Uncle and the rest of my warm little world. And I missed, how I missed, my own patch, my own front door, my own kitchen and all the things I'd gathered together in the short year since I'd moved into Sidi Daud, and most of all I missed our privacy.

Mrs Anderson was a wonder. At first I found it very hard to understand a word she said, for she spoke the 'Buchan', which is a strong Scottish accent with a lot of Gaelic words that I had to learn. She was also a real Scottish housewife and the lino everywhere was polished within an inch of its life, even under the multitude of little mats which adorned it. I discovered this quite easily the first time I came down the stairs with Christopher in my arms: arriving at the bottom, I set one foot on the mat and away we went, Christopher and I, and fetched up six feet away hard up against the front door.

The village had no electricity: it was promised, but hadn't arrived yet. We were all to be connected to the Grampian Hydro-Electric Scheme, and the poles would reach us in due course. So the first purchases we made in Hector Kidd's store were a tall Tilley lamp for the table and another, a storm lantern which we could use anywhere else, outside or inside. For cooking, how I missed my beautiful new gas stove, which stayed behind in Sidi Daud together with my prized instant water heater. Francis bought me a primus stove, which is, of course, a pressure stove, and a Blueflam, also run on kerosine, but not pressurised, and so cooks very gently. Mrs Anderson could cook practically anything on hers, including girdle scones and oat cakes. She taught me to make girdle scones, but she never succeeded in teaching me to make those wretched brittle oat cakes.

What with my very limited experience of cooking, and the little that was available to a family with only two and a half ration books, and now on top of that the necessity to cook meals on a Primus and a Blueflam, my first efforts at cooking were not all that successful, but after a while things improved, and Mrs Anderson taught me all manner of local dishes, like stovies, which is the Scottish for the French étuvés, a remnant of the time some call the Grand Alliance, and others think of as France's determined effort to take over Scotland for the French crown. Several items of food had names derived from the French; a leg of lamb was a 'gigot' and a fillet was always a 'filet'. I had a lot of learning to do.

Staying with Mrs Anderson at that time were her daughter and her husband; I saw very little of them, and I can't say I minded very much. They seemed a surly couple, and from what was not said, weren't too well liked in the village. Also staying in the house was Jamie Grant, who was a student at Torphins School during the week, but who went back to his own home, a remote croft, for the weekends. Jamie was learning to play the pipes, and every evening after his homework was done he would sit by the fire with Mrs Anderson and practise his music, just using the chanter, which brought the sound down to what was acceptable indoors. When he felt he had the tune right, he'd fit the chanter back into the pipes, go outside into the dark, and play, marching up and down the long drive that went past our bedroom window, and right down to the end of the garden. Up and down he'd march, up and down, and then when one of the twiddly bits gave him trouble, he'd stop just under our bedroom window and go over and over it until he got it right. Inevitably this would happen soon after I had put Christopher to bed and he had gone off to sleep, and just as inevitably he would wake up, screaming at the unfamiliar noise.

Our stay with Mrs Anderson was surprisingly short. Not long before Christmas, she came to Francis and me.

"I've some news for you," she said, "The Council are going to build a few prefabricated houses in that wee nook they cut out of the edge of the forest on to William Street. There'll be something like ten of them, and they'll be giving them to people who've come back from the war. Why don't you put your names down for one?"

"But, Mrs Anderson," I said, "won't they be for Torphins people? We've only just arrived here."

"No," she said, "Francis, you must go and see Councillor Laing, and talk to him about it. He's a fine man. He's retired now, but he used to be an Inspector of Police. He lives on the main road, no distance at all."

Francis walked round to Inspector Laing's house and talked the matter over with him. The Inspector urged Francis to put in an application, saying that the houses would be allocated on a points system, that service in the forces would earn so many points, service overseas would earn so many more, a wife would bring another few and a child some more. "In fact," he told Francis, "I think you might have a good chance, what with your years of service, and your wife's."

We owe a great deal to Mrs Anderson, and to Inspector Laing. When the applications were sorted out, we were allocated Number 5.

The houses went up very quickly indeed. It seemed that one day they weren't there and the next day there was this little cluster of ten houses on the big empty place between William Street and the beginning of the forest. And one of them would be ours!

The prefabs were wonders of planning: they contained a large living room, two bedrooms, the larger with built-in cupboards and drawers, a kitchen with electric stove, electric clothes boiler, a big double sink, a table that you could lower flat against the wall and a food cupboard. There was a bathroom and separate loo. The garden was small, but enough to plant quite a lot of vegetables and flowers, and have a small lawn, and there was also a shed.

Before we could move in we needed furnishings, carpet and curtains for the sitting room and some sort of carpet for the bedroom and nursery and curtains for those rooms, too. Francis undertook to attend to choosing all that, as it would all have to be ordered in Aberdeen, and having Christopher I wasn't very mobile. There were only four trains a day each way and about the same number of buses, and having to spend hours away from home with a breast-fed baby and nappies - well, it's inconvenient, to put it mildly.

Francis did us proud; his taste was excellent. The carpet men arrived and laid the carpets which, of course, I hadn't seen, and I was absolutely delighted. The fitted sitting room carpet was a rusty red, with a slight squiggly pattern in cream; the curtains, which were full length, were beige, with scattered flowers in the same cream, rusty red and green; the bedroom was carpeted in thick felt in soft green, and the curtains and bedspread were also green. There was also a brown and cream carpet for the nursery.

When Francis returned home after being demobbed he brought with him a mountain of stuff. There was the oak hunting chest, originally intended for storing guns and ammunition. It was lovely with elaborate dove-tailed corners and carved panels of a stag and acorns and oak leaves. He also brought the antlers of the red deer he had shot to feed the regiment. They had hung in a doleful row down that long passage in Sidi Daud, and were now in Mrs Anderson's shed. He had also brought three red deer skins, in full winter coat, with a thick ruff of fur round the necks. The skins had been cured, and we laid them on the green bedroom carpet. They just made that room, bringing a touch of luxury, even exoticism, that pleased us both. It was also very comforting, on bitter winter nights, when Christopher woke and cried, to be able to patter to the nursery with my bare feet sinking deep into that warm fur.

The nursery carpet was a warm, serviceable nut brown, and I made green curtains for the window, to match those in the kitchen. There was a bank of built-in drawers too in the nursery with a cupboard over them. What more could any young family want?

When all was ready, we hired Geordie and his railway lorry, which delivered coal and all sorts of farm supplies to the district, to bring our furniture from Mrs Anderson's shed round the corner to our new home. It was the week before Christmas.

We were in the nick of time: we had hardly moved into our new home when the weather closed in, and the days were shorter than ever. We hurried to get our fuel in, thinnings out of the forest, and Francis made a saw horse, and bought a bushman's saw to cut the wood into 'cloggies' about eight inches long. I tried to help him, but I am left-handed and he uses his right, and the results were not very effective. He accused me of twisting the saw and I accused him of the same thing, so I left him to do the job himself, which he did, very efficiently, well wrapped up and wearing his leather army jerkin and gloves.

The only weak bits of planning in the house were the steel outside wall in the bathroom and adjoining loo; the water pipe to the loo was attached to it and to stop it from freezing, I kept a tiny oil lamp, which I had had in the army, burning beneath it.

There was another weak spot: it was the outside wall in the sitting room, under the windows, which was also steel, and could have drained the heat out of the room however warm it was. We stacked all the cut cloggies along the outside of this wall, right up to window height, and they made a wonderful insulation. Once lit, we seldom let the fire go out. During the day time, we opened the doors, let the heat radiate into the room and enjoyed the sight of the dancing, ever-changing flames. At night we shut the fire doors and damped the fire down, and heat went through the ducts into the bedrooms.

By the time we moved in, the Grampian Hydro-Electric Scheme had reached the village, but not our little cluster of prefabs. As they were all-electric, we were very glad of the solid fuel fire, and of our kerosine lamps and stoves. Preparing for the cold, we laid in a small sack of oatmeal and a sack of potatoes. If we were marooned, we wouldn't starve.

Francis set about the garden, clearing the bracken and levering the boulders out of the black peaty soil of the remnants an ancient moraine. The tool he used was a tramp pick. This was a strong crowbar about four and a half feet long, with one end curved like half a pick axe, the other end with a wooden cross-bar handle. Low on one side there was a bar protruding which formed a stirrup for pushing the point of the pick into the ground with all the weight he could apply to his foot. Having loosened a rock from the ground, it could be so heavy that he needed my help to roll it away into the edge of the forest. At the back and the front he planted lawn and the area at the side of the house he turned into a kitchen garden. The soil was so acid it stained his hands black and few vegetables would grow without massive applications of lime.

Electricity came to our little group of houses just after Christmas: it was a great joy, and to cap it all, the council delivered the refrigerators which were designed to fit into the kitchen. We made all sorts of silly jokes about the refrigerator having been installed to keep the butter soft, but it did make such a difference. Cooking was a joy on the electric stove and we stacked our oil stoves away with very little regret.

The University year had begun in October. Francis caught the two minutes past seven train every morning and arrived back at two minutes past seven in the evening. The train took exactly one hour to do the Aberdeen-Torphins journey, so he had two whole undisturbed hours to study every day. For six months he never saw Torphins in the light except at weekends: it was dark every morning when he left and it was dark when he got back. Winter days in the north of Scotland are short: it wasn't full daylight until nine in the morning, and it was getting dark again by half past three.

So all day, every day, except for the weekend, I was alone with Christopher. I got to know people - there's nothing like pushing a pram for making friends. I got to know Hector Kidd who ran the shop - it was a big place for a small village. On one side there was a long counter, edged at the front with sacks of apples and potatoes and onions, with glass-topped tins of biscuits above them. On the other side of the shop was an equally long wooden counter, where farm supplies could be ordered, and where Hector had for sale everything you can imagine, from saucepans, chicken pellets, tea and dinner services, beehive parts and seed potatoes to the hefty pullovers and corduroy trousers that Francis bought when his battledress finally wore out.

CHAPTER 20

WINTER 1946-47

That winter was bitter, colder than I had ever known. Frost took the whole countryside in its pitiless grip and the earth froze as hard as iron. The farmers' clamps, where the potato crop lay, warmly bedded down in straw, and with two feet of earth over them, were too iced up to open. I found the hard way that nappies straight from the clothes boiler, and gently steaming as I hung them up, by lunch time resembled small sheets of frosted glass; when I peeled them carefully off the line and brought them into the kitchen, they thawed and collapsed into soggy heaps. This was catastrophic but, as usual, Francis solved the problem: we had a big airing cupboard, warmed by the hot water tank at the back of the fire and I hung the nappies from its slatted shelves. The warmth certainly helped, but when we stood the Tilley hurricane lamp on the floor of the cupboard, clothes dried in no time at all. The lamp was well below the clothes: it was not dangerous and gave us no trouble.

"It'll be warmer when the snow comes," said Hector one day, when I was giving him my order and trying to rub some life into my fingers, "You'll feel the difference. It won't be long now."

The snow came gently: one morning daylight arrived even more reluctantly than usual; yellowish leaden skies hung low over the Hill of Fare, and that afternoon, daylight faded even earlier than usual. By three o'clock I had lit the lamps and was drawing the curtains when I noticed that snow had begun to fall; big, soft, feathery flakes were drifting down in the half light, landing on the windows and sliding down gently to settle on the window sill. I drew the curtains close and threw another log on the fire.

The sitting room was cosy; Christopher lay on his tummy on the cream hearth rug, playing with his teddy. He had begun to make efforts to crawl; any day now he would be moving. In anticipation of this we had just bought a fire screen of the old nursery type, with a thick brass rail round the top, excellent for warming little clothes. Now I knew that, when he did manage to move, he would be safe, and shielded from the fire. I went into the kitchen and drew the gingham curtains and shut out the wintry scene.

Coming back, I noticed that the wind had risen: it had begun to whine round the house and now it began rumbling in the chimney. Some time later I became aware of a faint pitter-pattering on the windows and I pulled back the curtains and peered out. It was fully dark, but I could see that the character of the snow had changed: the flakes were small and hard, and the wind was driving them against the window panes where they piled up on the sills. It was going to be a bad night, stormy, as they say in the north, and I wished Francis were home.

I gave Christopher his supper, a messy business, since he wanted to do it himself, and his evening feed; I buttoned him into his blue sleeping bag and tucked him into his cot, and then went into the kitchen to cook dinner for Francis and me. He would be cold and tired after the hour-long journey from Aberdeen. My timing was good: the table was laid, and dinner ready when the train clattered into the station, brakes squealing as the wheels locked on the icy rails.

Five minutes later he opened the kitchen door and tramped in, and I saw why he had come in that way: from head to feet he was covered with snow. Even in that short distance from the station it had caked thick on to the front of his coat and trousers. He stripped off in the kitchen, got himself into clean shirt, trousers and pullover, shook the dry snow from the clothes he had taken off, and hung them up. Then he came into the sitting room, holding out his hands to the blazing logs to thaw them out. Dinner over, he settled down to study while I washed up and tidied the kitchen. That done, I curled up in my chair by the fire and opened the book I had borrowed from Mr McKay's little library. As usual I dropped off to sleep immediately, and an hour later Francis woke me: "Wake up, sleepyhead! Bed time!"

I had that book from Mr McKay so long, that once when I was in his shop buying some baby oil, he said, "Mrs Smith, you've had a book out of the library for three months. Have you forgotten?" I said, "Well, no, I haven't, Mr McKay. I've wanted to read that book for a long time. I really do want to read it, but every evening when I sit down to read it I just fall asleep."

The weather continued arctic, and snow fell every day, till in our little close it was three feet deep, and Francis had to dig a pathway into the road, where our neighbours all worked together to clear the rest of the way to William Street.

Francis, who for seven years in the army, had been accustomed to the outdoor life, with plenty of fresh air during the night, was apparently unaffected by the snow, and kept our bedroom windows wide open, a practise of which I strongly disapproved, and took my revenge by insisting on taking over for my own use some of the warm striped blue and white pyjamas he'd bought in the Officers Shop. I had my own but his were more accommodating. He felt quite strongly that they did nothing to enhance my charms, but at last he conceded that they were a practical solution. He also most obligingly swept up that night's ration of snow which had drifted through the window on to the dressing table and the carpet.

With the coming of the snow I found an unforeseen difficulty: I couldn't push the pram through it. I felt uneasy at leaving Christopher asleep in his cot while I did the shopping, but what else could I do? I couldn't carry him.

As usual, Francis had the answer: what we needed was a sledge like those in Germany on which all small children were towed around. He would make me one.

By this time Christopher had a chair of his own. It wasn't the traditional high chair: England was still short of wood, and babies were given low chairs, with the usual trays in front. Francis built a sledge, and made four square holes in the deck to take the legs of the low chair. When I needed to go shopping I took its tray off, fixed the pram's harness to the back of the chair, and strapped Christopher in. Wearing the pram suit my mother had made and cocooned in cot blankets he kept beautifully warm, and didn't seem to mind the arctic temperatures. Francis screwed a large brass ring to the front of the sledge, and made me a pole with a leather loop for my hand, and at the other end a brass hook to engage the ring. We were ready for the worst, or almost the worst, that winter could throw at us.

In Torphins that sledge was the sensation of the year! Every woman I met on my way to Hector Kidd's stopped to admire, and soon every man I met stopped to see how it was made, and more men came round in the evenings to have a closer look, till by the end of the winter a little fleet of sledges had taken to the roads. What I could never understand was why, in that bleak part of Scotland, where snow lay for weeks if not months, nobody had ever dreamed up the idea before. The only mishap I had with the sledge was when one day I was hurrying to reach home before the next blizzard arrived. Rushing through the passage cut through the snowdrift to cross the road, I took the corner too sharply, overturning the sledge. Christopher, finding himself lying in the snowdrift, soft, but horribly cold, voiced his disapproval in the usual way, all the way home.

*   *   *

The Deeside Super-Special Express, with its single track with passing places for the four trains a day each way, ran through deep cuttings on its way from Aberdeen to Ballater, the end of the line and the railhead for Balmoral. It was used to arctic weather, and in addition to a big snow plough that could be hitched to the front of the locomotive, at various stations along the line the arctic freeze was tempered by great boxes of hot water for icy feet. The carriage door was opened, the station master intoned, "Mind your feet, gentlemen," everybody lifted up their feet and the long steel box was thrust in, and eager feet were lowered upon it.

Too bad that by the time Francis was travelling this custom had lapsed.

One night we had a real blizzard. The next morning, Francis, arriving on time for the 7.02 train to Aberdeen, met the Station master, in gold-scuppered cap and heavy overcoat, hands dug deep in his pockets.

"There'll no be a train this side of noon," he said, his breath making a cloud of steam, "They put the engine away for the night in its shed up at Ballater, and it's snowed in. They canna open the doors to get it out and then they'll have to get it to the snow plough. There's a few tons of snow to be shovelled away first, and then the plough's got to clear the lines."

I believe the railway recruited labourers in Aberdeen and managed to get them to Ballater by bus, and the line was cleared eventually. But when the train arrived, running down the long descent from the hills, it braked for Torphins platform, but the wheels locked screaming on the icy rails, and the train, unable to stop, skidded through the station, and came to a halt some quarter of a mile beyond the platform.

As the passengers plodded along the line and climbed up into the carriages, the driver leaned out from the footplate:

"Sorry, lads," he said, "I just couldna help it!"

Just as well it wasn't the terminus.

*   *   *

The cold apart, there were certain aspects of life in this North of Scotland village which were much more pleasant than in Hastings. True it was difficult to find fruit, which had been such an important part of our diet, but now and again Hector seemed to be able to spare me a little more butter and cheese, and Mr Park the butcher, seemed able to give me a little more than the tiny meat ration that was all I'd ever got in the South. The height of my delight came one dark, snowy evening when I heard a knock at the kitchen door. I opened it and peered out:

"Mistress Smith," came a boy's voice from the dark, "My Dad's told me to tell you that a wee piggie's deid, and are you wanting a wee bittie pork?" Was I ever!

I never knew how that could have been worked. The dreaded Man From The Ministry always presided over the accouchements of pigs. The litters were registered straight away, and as far as I knew the same official presided over their conversion into pork. So how anyone managed to rear and despatch an unregistered piggie was a mystery, but the wee bittie pork, delivered next night, also under cover of darkness, was wonderful.

Another happening showed me just how far north of London we were, and how little the Ministry in Whitehall appreciated the climatic difference. Two staple foods we bought in bulk, following local practice. One was oatmeal, which we bought by the sack from Hector, and potatoes, which we bought from Jimmie who brought our milk. Potato harvesting took place in October, when the school was closed for a week so that the children could go and work at the 'tattie howking'. The potatoes were then laid in deep straw-lined trenches, well below the frost level, covered with more straw and the clamps filled in. There the potatoes could be safe from the worst weather, and the clamps could be opened to remove any quantity, provided the temperature was high enough for no frost to get at the crop.

The weather was at its most arctic when Jimmie received official notice from the Man from the Ministry that he was to open his clamps and remove some of his crop for shipment by rail to the south of England. In vain did Jimmie protest that if he opened his clamps in this weather the whole lot would be frosted and rot: the Word of the Ministry had gone forth. Jimmie came to me almost in tears. Once opened in that weather, he couldn't remake the clamp - everything would go bad. Would I please buy a sack of potatoes? Of course, we did, and joined the song of hate against south of England bureaucrats who hadn't a clue and cared less. The consignment of potatoes which went by rail was frosted and rotten by the time it reached London.

That winter the heavy falls of snow buried many sheep in the fields. Like any animals, they went to shelter in dips in the ground, going downhill until stopped by fences or hedges, and there the snow buried them. They could breathe: to some extent snow is porous, but when the small amount of grass they could reach was finished, they could starve and many did. The RAF flew bales of hay from Dyce airport and dropped them over the farms, and this must have saved hundreds.

That was a terrible winter. I was unused to such low temperatures, and winter seemed to go on and on as though it would last for ever, with no relief from its icy grip, not the smallest sign of spring. I was very glad of the Harris tweed suit I'd bought when I was demobbed, and of the warm overcoat that went over it. Francis bought me a pair of men's Beaver boots, and hammered nails like trefoils all over the soles, to give me some grip on the icy roads, and I managed very well, with a pair of his socks over my stockings. But when, oh when would this winter come to an end?

It ended eventually; imperceptibly the days began to lengthen. But the snow was lying just as deep when we had the worst blizzard of all. It caught me with Christopher on his sledge in William Street, only a few hundred yards from home and shelter, but I couldn't make it. The wind screamed down the road towards us, and with it came the snow, frozen hard and driving like needles into our faces, blotting out all sight of houses and even of the road ahead. We could have been alone in a boundless desert of snow. I stopped, unhooked the pole and stood with my back to the wind, opened my overcoat and held it round the child. How long I stood like that I have no idea; it seemed hours before the wind slackened and I could dare to turn round and face forward, hook up the sledge and finish our short journey home.

I had never been very keen on snow, but never before had I realised just how deadly such weather can be and how real had been the emergency that sent late revellers at Hogmanay to look for two men who had not returned home from their celebrations. They were found sleeping peacefully in a snowdrift, were wakened up and helped home, where their welcome probably brought them back to life more quickly than anything else. In that cold, they'd have been dead by morning.

Spring came at last, weeks after it had arrived in the south of England. I thought longingly of the springs of my childhood, with the bursting into life of trees and flowers, of the primroses and violets, the sweet new green of the trees, drifts of bluebells in the woods, orchards full of apple blossom. This was a different country, harder, much harder, but so beautiful when eventually spring arrived. Days were lengthening, the sun shone with gentle warmth, nappies no longer froze on the line, and Christopher was crawling at top speed all over the house.

And with the spring, Francis's ideas of a hobby, some way of supplementing our small allowance of £7 a week, burgeoned. He had always wanted to keep bees, always been interested in them, ever since Great Uncle Hugh had kept hives on Dartmoor. I wasn't so keen on the idea, not that I'd had much to do with bees, or any other insects, for that matter. As a three-year old child, staying in Oxshot one summer I'd been stung by a wasp, and I hadn't forgotten it. We'd been sitting in the dining room, having afternoon tea. It was a hot day, the windows stood wide open, and a wasp, that spoiler of English picnics, was hovering round a dish of jam. A moment later I felt a tickling behind my ear and put up my hand. It was the wasp and it stung me, and I roared. After that, somehow, bees, wasps, all those things, were, as far as I was concerned, OUT.

So it was a pity that Francis should be so taken with bees, and that he was prepared to invest good money in hives and the makings for frames, and nails and wire, smokers, veils and all sorts of bits and pieces to further his interest. He assured me he'd be able to make quite a bit of money, which would help while he was studying, but I wasn't convinced.

Travelling every day to Aberdeen he had also met a local beekeeper. They became great friends, and Alastair taught him a lot about keeping bees in that locality. And Francis being Francis, bought books on the subject and swotted the subject up, just as if it had been one of his subjects at university.

CHAPTER 21

BEES AND BABIES

After that bitter winter, Francis and his beekeeping friend, Alastair, decided that any bees that had survived would be of good strain and free from disease. Bees were hard to come by that spring. Many colonies had died during the winter, but an elderly man who lived further up the valley at Dinnet, wanted to reduce the number of his hives. He had the reputation of being a very good beekeeper and Francis was recommended to buy. So Francis went to the roup and bought his first hive of bees.

It was a massive white-painted construction with legs, a flight board, and a gabled roof, an absolute bee palace. The bees were very quiet, and though we put them in the garden, close to where I was constantly passing by to hang out the laundry or doing a little gardening, they gave no sign of resenting us. In fact, one afternoon I found Christopher bent in two, poking a stick in the entrance, and the bees simply queueing up behind him, waiting for him to move so that they could deliver their loads of nectar.

A few days later, however, our little cat Binti, who had made the transfer from Hastings with very little trouble, got the first sting of her young life inspecting that same entrance. Suddenly she sprang vertically two feet into the air, every hair stood on end, and with her tail like a flue brush, she shot round the corner of the house and vanished. It was two hours later when she reappeared, very subdued.

We had great fun with that hive. We opened it up quite often, just to see how the bees were getting on, and we even got quite fond of the queen, whom we called Aggie.

But now Francis, who could read an Ordnance Survey map before he could read the written word, discovered the apiary site of his dreams. It was up in the hills beyond Torphins, on the lower slopes of the Hill of Fare, a wide, sheltered valley with a small stream running through it. He went in search of the farmer, and found him, a grand biblical figure, well over six feet tall, striding around one of his fields, sowing oats in awkward areas. He was broadcasting the seed with wide sweeps of his arm from a kidney shaped basket slung in front of him, his long white beard blowing in the wind. Francis asked if he might put a few hives in what was obviously an unused patch of the farm, 'alongside the burn.' He roared with laughter and boomed, "You can put them in the burn if you've a mind."

The farm was called Fordie, and so Fordie Apiaries was born. The plural was a bit of a joke, but as Francis said, it did leave room for expansion.

Then Francis bought six more hives. They came 'in the flat' which means they had to be put together and then he had to assemble the frames and put in the comb foundation. I thought them pretty uninteresting compared with that Rolls Royce of a hive which now decorated the front garden, standing on the patch of lawn we had sown. When these new hives were assembled, they just looked like a collection of boxes, but Francis seemed pleased with them. From somewhere in Fife he bought six straw skeps of Dutch bees and transferred the bees to his new hives. We were all set to start up Fordie Apiaries. Then we hit a major snag: how were we, with no transport, to get the hives up to Fordie?

He solved that problem by taking the wheels off his bicycle, and using them to build what Torphins called a 'hurley'. With this little hand-cart it was no trouble at all to ferry the new hives up to Fordie. In fact, the hurley became essential to running the bees; there was always something that had to be taken up or brought back.

Whenever I could, I helped Francis. As far as I can remember, the bees were so gentle that I didn't bother with a veil or gloves, and it was at Fordie that I got my first sting since the wasp stung me all those years ago at Oxshot. I didn't bother about it: Francis scraped the sting out, and that was that. Then the palms of my hands began to itch - I'd been stung on the hand - and I felt a bit queer, but it passed, and I thought no more about it.

The next time I was helping Francis at Fordie, a bee became entangled in my hair, and when I tried to get it out, it stung my head. This time there was a definite reaction. My body itched, and big white weals began to appear on my arms and legs. Francis unbuttoned my shirt and found that back and front, I was covered with weals. It was a general reaction. I felt shaky, and Francis packed up what he was doing and slowly we made our way home. By the time we reached home, a sort of adrenalin reaction had set in; I was excited and felt like rushing around and working at top speed. Francis soon put a stop to that, sat me down and made me a cup of tea. The excitement and the weals subsided and vanished.

That was the last time I was stung in Scotland, and I don't think either of us really understood that I had been given a warning: the next time would be much worse. I had, in fact, developed a hyperallergy to bees, triggered by that first sting when I was only three years old. At that time there was a theory that taking calcium tablets would help the condition and dutifully I worked through packets of them, but from what happened later on they can't have made much difference.

Looking back on those days, I realise that the people who had lived in Torphins all their lives found our goings-on very interesting. Here was an army officer, just demobbed, with no delusions of grandeur at all, studying at the university, working in the forest in his holidays and setting up a beekeeping business to help himself through college. They were sympathetic and most helpful. Possibly Francis gained additional sympathy because, while we had one of the smallest houses in the village, another Aberdeen University student had rented the biggest, a great, rambling, turreted, Victorian Gothic mansion called Craig Rannoch. We became friendly with John Robertson and with his wife, Mary, specially with Mary, who had also been in the army, and had a small son of Christopher's age.

In an odd way it was unfortunate for John that his military career had been so different from Francis's. When war broke out John was already at university, and so received a direct commission on enlisting. From there he had gone on to become the youngest brigadier in the British army, accustomed to authority and deference. Somehow he didn't go down so well in the village as did Francis, with his rural interests and complete lack of side.

Francis and I had thought that it would be nice to have another child, and for this one to be a summer baby, so that we could get over the early months in the good weather, but Rosemary decided not to wait for us to make up our minds, and Dr Morrison told us to expect her round about Christmas, another winter baby. Thank goodness at least I had learned to cope with nappies in the cold weather, and, after all, by the time she arrived Christopher would be nearly two.

In June Francis sat his exams, Physics, Chemistry, Zoology and Botany, and swam through the lot, with the exception of the Inorganic Chemistry, which he flunked, not really surprising, as he had never done it before. His school had banned the subject ever since an absent-minded teacher of chemistry had made a trifling error and blown up the school laboratory. So Francis had to study the subject in the long vacation, which was vexatious, with so many better things to do, but he did it and passed his re-sit. Looking back, he has a feeling that the high head ones were kind to him.

Fordie apiaries built up very well that year, and when the heather began to bloom, our hives were sitting right in the middle of the crop, and the air was heavy with the scent of honey.

In October Francis went back to university, and was soon immersed in his studies. The bees had been put to bed for the winter with ample stores, and there wasn't much to be done for them.

Snow began early that year, and by the beginning of December it was pretty deep. On the night of the 5th I woke in discomfort and realised that Rosemary had no intention of waiting for Dr Morrison's estimated date: she was on her way. My bag was packed and ready, and I was booked into the Cottage Hospital just round the corner, next to Mrs Anderson's house. I woke Francis.

"I think you'd better go over the bridge and wake Forbes Phillips, and ask him to bring the taxi. I need to go to hospital."

Francis got up and dressed with all the speed he'd learned under fire in Tobruk, shrugged into his felt jacket and was gone. I dressed and sat waiting. He was longer than I expected, but at last I heard him open the front door, kicking the snow from his boots.

"Have you brought the taxi?"

"The taxi's not there. There's not a car in the place. Even Dr Morrison's gone."

"But where are they? I can't walk. What are we to do?"

"Forbes' wife says the bus has skidded off the road. It's half buried in a snowdrift, some miles from here, and everyone with a car has gone to get the people out before they freeze. It's bitterly cold."

Then he had a brilliant thought. There was only one car left, too small to be called to go nobly to the rescue: it was Teddie Reid's fish van, a tiny two-seater truck painted dark green outside, and inside strongly perfumed with fish.

Big Teddie and Agnes and Wee Teddie, eleven years old, lived just across the way in another prefab. Francis went over the road and thundered on their door and eventually a sleep-soggy Big Teddie opened and peered out. Francis explained the emergency, and Teddie, too, did a quick change into outdoor clothes. In a matter of minutes the Fish Reid limousine was at the door and I was ushered into the passenger seat, as carefully as if I had been made of spun glass, and my bag slung into the back with the empty fish boxes. It only took a few minutes to deliver me to the hospital, and then both Francis and Teddie went back to bed and to sleep.

Rosemary was born two hours later, without the help of Dr Morrison, who was delivering his load of shivering bus passengers to their homes. On his return he looked in at the hospital, saw that all was well with Rosemary and me and then he, too, went back home to bed.

Next morning, on his way to catch the 7.02 am train for Aberdeen, Francis entered my room by way of the open window and met his daughter. What a nice easy way to have an addition to the family!

Later than morning, Dr Morrison, doing the family shopping, went into Teddie Reid's fish shop.

"Aye-aye, Dr Morrison," said Teddie in his newly acquired Scots accent, "Ye didna ken I was at the relief of Ladysmith, did ye?"

"No, Teddie," said Dr Morrison, stowing away his parcel of fish, and buttoning up his overcoat, "I wouldn't have thought you were old enough."

"Ah, but ye see," said Teddie, "that was just last night."

Rosemary proved to be my ideal baby, happy and contented and so much easier than Christopher had been. The great difficulty was in getting the nursery warm enough to bath her, as I did every morning at ten o'clock. Week after week the nursery windows were thick with ice and the room itself far too cold to undress her. Eventually

I did it in the sitting room in front of the fire, the fire doors open and a kerosine heater to help matters.

Christopher celebrated his second birthday, with a very small party; Mary Robertson brought her little son, Simon, and we had tea and sandwiches, the children drank their milk and played, we talked, and Rosemary lay in her carrycot and did nothing very much. Our friendship with Mary had become even closer since we discovered that Mary's parents, the Taylors, had not only known Francis's Uncle Lionel and Auntie Maud when they all lived in Tientsin, but were their best friends. The Taylors came up from London and stayed with John and Mary at Craig Rannoch, and it was good to be able to write to Uncle Lionel and tell him that we had met them.

It was time to arrange for Rosemary to be baptised, and she would need a godparent. Catholics were pretty thin on the ground in Aberdeen, but one of Francis's fellow students qualified and Francis 'volunteered' him. He was Maurice Mulcahy, who had spent the war in the Royal Navy and was now doing Forestry at Aberdeen. Neither he nor Francis had any transport, but Father Butler, the Parish Priest at Aboyne, nine miles west of Torphins ("He's English, but he's all right." said the Bishop's housekeeper), offered to pick us all up and take us to the church.

He had a small car, and we were a tight fit. Father Butler and Francis sat in the front, and Maurice, Christopher and I crammed into the back. We had set off and gone some way before I realised we had forgotten the baby. We remedied that. In the small church there was nobody but us, and when the ceremony was over, Father Butler ran us all back and we had tea and the cakes and sandwiches I had left ready.

It was in April, when Rosemary was four months old and the days were warmer and sunny, that Christopher discovered how to unlock the front door. He had already shown signs of being a wanderer, and every morning when I was ready to bath Rosemary and feed her, I had begun to lock both front door and kitchen door. The kitchen door had a lock and key: the front door, however, was fitted with some patent affair with a lever which switched to the locked position. There were no bolts to the door, and as for some reason the door was made of steel, we couldn't fit one.

I left Christopher playing happily on the nursery floor and had reached the stage of lowering Rosemary's tiny slippery body back into the water, when I suddenly realised I couldn't hear any sound from Christopher. I wrapped Rosemary in the towel, laid her back in her cot, covered her up, and went to investigate. He was gone, and the front door I had locked so carefully stood wide open.

I ran down the little garden path, looked both ways. Woodside Crescent was a cul-de-sac. The only way for him to go was towards William Street, which ran right and left at the end of our small enclave. It was only a few yards to the road. I ran up to the corner, looked down towards the croft at the end of the road: nothing - the road was completely empty. I turned, looked up towards the station and the bank and Mrs Anderson's. Nothing. My God, the railway line.

The village of Torphins is cut in two by the single track railway line from Aberdeen to Ballater. There are three ways to move from one side of the line to the other. The first, at the bottom of William Street and past the croft, goes under the line, the second, in the centre of the village, carries a busy road over the line, and then half way between the two is the little wooden footbridge which serves the station and all of us on our way to the shops. Which way had he gone?

Leaving the front door wide open, I ran round the house to the shed, pulled out my bike and pedalled out of the road, out into William Street, down to the croft, turned right under the bridge and carried on till I had worked my way to Hector Kidd's shop. Hector was standing outside, looking up the main road. He showed no surprise at seeing me flying along on my bike, hatless, coatless, and with my bathing apron still on. He just pointed up the road towards the station. "There he is: I told him to back to his Mummie, but all he said was 'Me's going for a walk.'"

I caught up with him, just as Mrs McLeod, whose small shop sold groceries and things like sock wool, came out and stopped the little figure. I heard her say, "Christopher, where's your Mummie?" I heard him answer, "Mummie's bathing my baby sister."

I put him on the bicycle saddle and wheeled him back home. The door still stood open. I dropped the bike and we went in. Rosemary was asleep and the bath water cold.

After that episode, the whole time I was tied up with Rosemary's routine I was on edge, constantly listening for him, and Christopher's next adventure I managed to cut short: I caught up with him on the little wooden footbridge over the line at the station. His urge to roam was making both Francis and me very anxious. Certainly, Torphins was a small village, and there were plenty of people who knew him, but that main road, carrying all the road traffic from Aberdeen to Ballater, could be dangerously busy, specially at the time of the Highland Games at Aboyne, just up the road, and the great Gathering at Braemar. Christopher might have all the confidence in the world, but no child of that age understands traffic. Telling him not to do it had no effect at all, and the front door was as much good as a mosquito net.

His next adventure was the worst, and it occurred as usual when I was bathing Rosemary. I heard a man's voice calling me from the front door; I laid down Rosemary and hurried into the hall. The door was wide open, and there standing on the mat was the railway signalman, holding Christopher firmly by the hand.

"I'm just working in my box, ye see, Mistress," he said, "and getting ready for the train and I look doon the line and there's this young skalliwag marching along between the rails as bold as brass! I canna stay: I'm awa'! The train's due in five minutes!" and he ran back down the road to the railway line, leaving me holding on to Christopher's hand for dear life. After that I tried pushing a chair beneath the door handle, and, thank goodness, it worked.

That summer the council decided to put fences round our gardens, with a gate at the side of the house. I breathed a sigh of relief: now Christopher could play in the garden and he'd be corralled.

No such luck. He stood and looked at the patent latch for perhaps five whole minutes, then unlocked the gate and walked out. Eighteen months later another child at the top of the road still hadn't worked it out.

Rosemary was only four months old when I became aware that I was going to have another child. To say I was upset is putting it mildly. Christopher took so much of my time, that it was lucky that Rosemary was placid. By then Rosemary would be crawling all over the place. How could I manage with another tiny mite? Francis solved it, as he solved most of our problems, by finding the daughter of one of the local farmers; she had also been in the army, and we took to each other straight away. She came in every weekday morning, did the housework, and helped me with the washing. It was marvellous, and life became worth living again. I could enjoy the children, and take them for walks, which seemed to keep Christopher's wanderlust under control.

Francis also decided that I should have a new pram, partly as a consolation prize for having the new baby so quickly, and partly because the old one, beautifully sprung, but high off the ground, was unstable in a high wind. We found that out the easy way.

One windy day, while I was entertaining an elderly and very proper neighbour with tea and cakes, Christopher decided to take his baby sister for a walk. He released the pram brake, and before he knew what had happened, the wind filled the hood and away went the pram with Rosemary inside it; it was stopped by colliding with a bush. The pram tipped up and stood on its hood, with Rosemary in a heap inside it, and her usual sunny disposition very much in abeyance.

The new pram was a Dunkley Duchess, deep blue, with a deep blue hood lined with cream; it was a low pram with small wheels, and provision for a toddler to have a lift. It had a beautiful canopy. It was elegant. Could any woman want more?

CHAPTER 22

HONEY SUMMER

The winter of 1947-48 was cold, and the snow lay for months. Just as the year before, the onset was sudden, but much more ferocious. The first we knew about it was when the radio gave us a blizzard warning, and that really rocked me. A blizzard! What did they call the snow storms we'd had last winter? They were pretty bad, but there had been no official blizzard warning. And how was I going to get to the shops? Rosemary was too small to go in Christopher's sledge: I'd have to leave her at home. And Christopher! He had grown so much, none of last winter's clothes would be of any use, and I had nothing warm enough for him to wear trotting about in such weather. Funds were short, and material to make him a snow suit would cost coupons, too.

I solved it. When Francis came out of the army he bought himself some extra grey army blankets; he brought home seven of them. As blankets they had come in very handy, but we didn't need all of them. Or if we did, too bad: one of them was going to be sacrificed! I hurried to Mrs McLeod's shop and bought a snow suit pattern. It was all in one, from hood to ankles, and it did up in front with a long zip. That evening when Christopher and Rosemary were asleep, and Francis deep in his studies, I spread out one of Francis's blankets on the carpet and cut out the snow suit. I got out my ancient sewing machine - it had been my grandmother's and was feeling its age - and settled down to make it up. I lined the hood with some fine woollen material cut from a piece I'd bought to make myself a skirt. The skirt could wait: this couldn't. Some time after midnight I finished the whole thing, complete with zip and knitted cuffs at the wrists and ankles.

Before I laid the little snow suit over a chair and went yawning off to bed, the wind was rumbling in the chimney and I could hear the thrashing of the trees in the wood behind the house. Then came that metallic noise of frozen snow slamming against the windows. The predicted blizzard had arrived: I was just in time with Christopher's suit.

Next morning, when I opened the door for Francis to go to the station the wind had risen to gale force and the air was filled with whirling frozen snow. It was already inches deep on the ground. Later that morning, when Rosemary, bathed and fed, was asleep in her cot, I dressed Christopher in his new snow suit and little yellow gum boots and we started out to walk to the shops, over the little foot bridge. He was delighted with himself, and not only showed his blanket suit to everyone we met, but was reluctant to let me take it off when we reached home again.

The storm continued for several days; snow lay deep underfoot and we had to shovel a way down the garden path and out into the road. The temperature was well below freezing and I was very glad to have the kerosine lamp in the airing cupboard for drying nappies. Each morning Francis went off to university well rugged up in his American felt jeep jacket, and his British leather jerkin over it and his trousers tucked into those wonderful battle dress boots-cum-gaiters. It was a relief they were lasting so well.

Then the worst happened. Somewhere the snow and the gale combined and brought down the main power lines to Torphins. The whole village was without power. I never found out where it had actually happened: I was too busy coping with the results. We had no power at all. We had no lights, no heating, no power for cooking, no electric boiler, no electric iron. It was back to the bad old days of the Tilley lamps and the hurricane lamp, the Primus and the Blueflam. I was furious! This was awkward for me; and how thoughtless people were to allow me to be deprived of my electricity! It was not long since the house had been connected to the Grampian Hydro-Electric Scheme but how quickly we had accustomed ourselves to it, had come to take for granted having power at the touch of a switch.

Unwillingly, and because we had to, we unearthed all the kerosine appliances from the back of the cupboard. We stood the Primus and the Blueflam on the useless stove and went back to soups and stews. I discovered that the kerosine iron had its advantages: it had no cord to dangle and catch my foot in. And what a very mellow light those Tilley lamps threw, and we could put them just where we needed the light. We even bought a trivet for the sitting room fire: it fitted over the bars of the grate and the kettle sat on it and boiled in no time at all.

It was more than a week before the power lines were repaired and the kerosine appliances returned to the bottom of the hall cupboard, and this time I had a few faint regrets, but on the other hand, who really likes cleaning lamp glasses? But we kept the trivet.

In the spring I had a letter from my father, telling me that my stepmother's mother had died. The protracted illness had taken a great toll of my mother; it had damaged her heart, and she must now take things quietly for a while. They were thinking of moving down to Worthing, where they would look for a house near the sea, somewhere with less hills than Carshalton. In early summer they decided to make their first ever visit to Scotland. They were also, I think, rather anxious to see in what sort of conditions we were living. As we had only the two bedrooms, both fully occupied, they stayed at Bridge House, a small and very nice private hotel a few minutes away.

It was wonderful to see them; I hadn't realised how much I missed them, in spite of the separations of the war years. As we neared the house, my father stopped outside, his hands in his pockets, inspecting it, and was non-committal, but when he went inside, and saw how we had furnished it, and how comfortable it was, he said that it was a 'pretty good shed', and after that he always called our home 'the shed'.

They stayed with us for two weeks, and never did two weeks fly so fast. Just before they left, the farmer at Fordie asked Francis if he would like him to grow our potatoes for us. If we gave him a bag of seed potatoes (bought from Hector Kidd) and took them up to the farm, they could be planted and grown with his, and we would pay him in potatoes, one row for him and one for us. It was a good idea; Francis bought a sack of seed potatoes and put them on the hurley and left it outside the house, ready to push up to Fordie.

A little later I went into the kitchen to start cooking lunch, and found my father standing motionless at the window, gazing up the road. I joined him.

"What are you looking at, Daddy?"

"If I hadn't seen it with my own eyes, I shouldn't have believed it. I still don't believe it," he said. Then I saw what he was watching. Halfway up the road was our three-year-old son, pushing the hurley with its load of a hundredweight of potatoes. I made for the door;

"Really, Daddy, you might have stopped him. I never know what that child's going to do next."

Mummie and Daddy left us and returned south. We waved goodbye at the station and went back home, silently.

*   *   *

By now we had twenty hives near the burn at Fordie. That spring was wonderful, and the bees built up into strong colonies. They found food from the sycamores, the lime trees and the hedge flowers. Francis had ideas never before tried out in that part of the world. He intended to practise migratory beekeeping, as was done in Australia.

He would take the bees to every major honey crop within reasonable reach, rather than wait for the honey crop to come to the bees. He had bought himself a light motor bike and on this he hunted around for an area with a very early flowering crop.

He found it near Brechin, in Strathmore, south of Torphins, where he contacted a man who grew raspberries commercially. They came to an agreement that Francis should bring his bees and position them on his land in time for the raspberries' flowering. Francis would get the honey and the bees would fertilise the raspberry flowers, and so give the farmer an increased yield of fruit.

It worked very well indeed. In May, Francis hired the railway lorry, which had a platform back, and he and Geordie loaded the hives and drove through the early dawn light over the Cairn-na-Mount road to the farm, where they set out the hives, removed the wire travelling screens and the entrance blocks which had confined the bees for the journey and returned home. Now that Francis had his own transport he could pay regular visits to the hives to check that all was well.

The bees stayed there till midsummer day, by which time most of the flowering was over and the fruit set. That evening he drove back to Brechin. He removed box after box of beautiful pale honey, stacked them and bound them with steel tape. He took off the roofs and replaced them with the travelling screens. Then he had to wait for the bees to stop flying for the night so that he could put in the entrance blocks. He had to wait a long time: at midsummer in the north of Scotland the night is very short; at midnight it is light enough to read a newspaper. Francis made himself comfy lying on the stacked boxes and slept. Four hours later, as dawn brought colour back into the world, came Geordie in the lorry. They loaded up the hives already prepared for travelling and came back to Torphins, unloading them at Fordie in their accustomed place. It was so well timed that the clover in the surrounding farms was just coming into flower, pastures of white clover and pastures of purple. The scent was rich and sweet, and the bees set to work with a will.

What a year that was. We now owned an extractor and a settling tank, and we extracted the raspberry honey in the kitchen. We had also invested in bottles for the crop and Francis had had printed a rather distinctive label. The one we used now said, "FORDIE APIARIES FINEST RASPBERRY HONEY". The honey went like hot cakes. We were in production, and Francis had finished his end of the year exams.

The clover flowers in the pastures withered, the glorious, evocative scent faded, and the bees processed and stored honey of the palest yellow, capping it with the thinnest, whitest wax. The boxes of honeycomb, each one perfect, were removed from the hives, brought home in the hurley and uncapped with a water-heated knife, in the kitchen. The honey was beautiful. We strained it and bottled it, and put our own yellow and black label on the bottles, "PURE CLOVER HONEY FORDIE APIARIES".

Then Francis transferred all the hives to the Forest of Birse, which is a grouse moor. I doubt if there is one tree, but miles of purple heather, bell and ling. It was lovely up there, so quiet, except for the birds, and the sound of the wind, soughing through the heather, and the sky was enormous, and bounded only by hills. The bell heather flowered first and then the ling, and it looked as though we'd have a big crop.

At this juncture, Francis, all studying over for the year, was due to go with the other students of his Year to spend a fortnight in Normandy, to examine the splendidly run French State Forests. Before he left, he put ample boxes on the hives, so that however much honey the bees brought in, there would be plenty of room and they would not be tempted to swarm. The children and I waved him goodbye at the station, the train swept out of sight round the bend and I walked back home with Rosemary in her beautiful pram, Christopher helping me push it. I don't think Rosemary was affected, but both Christopher and I felt decidedly flat.

Life went on as usual, quite well, in fact, though the evenings were lonely, and all was well until a few days before Francis was due to return. Then, one morning, the postie came, and instead of pushing my letters through the letter box, he knocked at the door. "Aye-aye, Mistress Smith," he began, "I've a message for you from the postie at Banchory. Mr MacDonald, the ghillie at the Forest of Birse, asked him to let you know that your bees are wanting tae swarm out: there's so much honey coming in they havena enough room. You'll need to be going up there and taking some more boxes, and a hive, too, I'm thinking."

I thanked him, and went back to the sitting room and slumped in a chair. What on earth was I to do? I'd no transport, and it was miles and miles to the Forest of Birse. And there'd be boxes and an extra hive to take and a smoker and fuel and all sorts of things. I walked across to share my troubles with Agnes.

"What'll I do?" I wailed, "These things always happen when Francis isn't here."

"Well," said Agnes, "We'll ask Big Teddie when he comes in. If you can cope with the bees, I know he'll drive you. I'll look after the bairns. Wee Teddie's old enough to look after himself."

Bless Agnes, but cope with the bees? I was not so sure that I could cope, specially if some of them had already swarmed out, but something had to be done and quickly, before Francis lost the bees and the honey, too, if other hives started robbing.

That evening Big Teddie drove me in the fish van up to the the Forest of Birse, the perfumed interior of the van loaded with a spare hive and extra boxes. We drove through Banchory, past the salmon ladder where we usually lingered, and up on to the grouse moor. Just as we reached the bees, we met Mr MacDonald, the ghillie. He was a man with the beautiful manners and gentle voice of the true highlander, and he was psychic, too. Well, he must have been, for as I unloaded boxes and a sheet and the rest of the gear, he looked straight into my craven soul and said, "Mistress, are you wanting to do it yourself, or would you be liking me to give you a hand?"

The wonderful man! One hive had already sent out a swarm. He laid the sheet down before the empty hive I had brought with me, shook the swarm on to it and as we watched the bees run up and into the hive we spotted the long golden brown body of the queen and knew the bees would stay. He put an extra box on all the hives: they were beginning to look like bee skyscrapers. While the swarm was running up the cloth and into the empty hive, a number of bees flew around and landed on his hairy Harris tweed jacket, which he hadn't bothered to remove. If there's one thing bees can't stand it's hairy tweed. One adventurous bee made its way up the jacket and down between his neck and his open shirt. I'd have screamed the place down. All he said was, "Bide a wee, bide a wee,"and very gently, removed the bee with his finger. It didn't sting him. I've often thought about Mr MacDonald who did, all unprotected, what certainly I and most probably Francis couldn't have done without protection. It was due, I think, to his utter gentleness.

Francis returned that weekend, glad to be home, but having spent an interesting time in the French forests. He was amazed to hear that I had had to take extra boxes and a hive up to the grouse moor, and on his motor bike he paid a rapid visit to see how things were. The flowering of the heather was already waning, he said, and it wouldn't be too long before we could bring the hives down and start extracting. Scottish heather honey is greatly prized, and should fetch a good price on the market. There was only one snag, he said; it was thixotropic - it was difficult to persuade it to come out of the combs, where it set in a thick jelly, and needed stirring up before it would flow out into the extractor.

He bought the tool for doing this. It was a block of wood set with three inch nails, points up, at just the right interval to fit into the middle of each cell of a comb. You plunged it up and down a few times, and the honey became liquid. I know now that that tool was in fact a hackle, such as is used for combing fleece before hand spinning it. I've got one myself for just that purpose.

The crop from the heather was so heavy that we knew I could never have the time to help him. Rosemary was nine months old and crawling, and between the two children I had plenty to do, so Francis persuaded Maurice Mulcahy and other students to come and give him a hand. They slogged away in the kitchen, extracting, and I provided beer and food. They did a magnificent job, and when all the extracting was done, and the sticky combs returned to the hives for the bees to clean up, Francis and I were left with gallons of high grade honey, which we'd have to sell.

We had scooped the market with the early honey, the raspberry and the clover. Now to sell the precious heather honey. If it had been a good year for our bees at the heather, it would have been the same for every other beekeeper in that part of Scotland. The local market would be flooded. We must look elsewhere. We devised an advertisement and sent it to the *Times* of London.

"Glorious heather honey from Royal Deeside", it ran, "10/- a pound jar. Apply Fordie Apiaries, 5 Woodside Crescent, Torphins, Aberdeenshire."

Shs 10/- was an astronomical price, but we were flooded out with orders. I think the advertisement must have appealed to the snob latent in most of us.

Having seen how radios and such delicate ware were treated, we ordered special packaging for the bottles to withstand the ferocity of the porters at the London train termini, and most of the honey arrived safely, but in spite of the packaging some jars were broken and these we replaced, but on the whole everything went well and our bank balance grew a little healthier.

It was just as well. I was expecting the new baby early in January, and that made three little people to be fed and clothed on our tiny £7 a week grant.

It was during this summer and the lovely autumn which followed that I began to feel bloody-minded. Francis was working hard at University, he was in daily contact with interesting people, and doing things which made him use his brain. I, on the other hand, having used my brain just as hard as I could all the war, now found myself constricted to the role of wife, mother, nurse, cook, housekeeper, gardener and laundry maid, specially the laundry maid. It began to irk me. It was probably jealousy, that nasty mordant pest. Ever since we were married we'd never had a decent period to be together, just our two selves, with no children demanding constant attention, and with no studying to take up spare time. It niggled me: *I* wanted some attention; *I* wanted to do interesting things: *I* wanted a bit of adult conversation. I was fed up with feeds of sloppy stuff that went all over bibs and high chairs and the floor, I was fed up with nappies, and with the prospect of lots more to come. Poor Francis, he had a thin time.

I got over it, of course. As my pregnancy advanced it was enough to get through the day, even with the help of Betty, who continued to be a strong right arm. But at Christmas Betty told me, sadly, that she'd have to leave. She was getting married in the new year. She'd miss me, she said, and I knew I'd miss her. She left, and I was devastated.

Mrs Anderson found me someone else. She was a Niven, and I knew her elder sister, a hulking lump of a girl, not very bright nor prepossessing. The younger girl, Morag, had just left school, and Mrs Anderson reckoned that if I kept a firm hand on her she'd be all right.

She wasn't. She was the laziest girl of her age I ever came across, and I felt I could trust her just as far as I could throw her. But what to do? If she could at least take the children off my hands while I worked, and again while I rested in the afternoon perhaps I could manage.

Christmas and Hogmanay came and went. On the night of the 10th January, I woke Francis - why do these things happen at night? - and announced that I was off to the hospital, and it was such a glorious night that we could walk there, and not bother Forbes Phillips.

We started out strolling and finished at a smart trot. I had barely time to say goodbye to Francis before dashing into the hospital and gasping "Quick!" David was born half an hour later, a small baby, under six pounds, and looking displeased with the whole process. The business was over by the time Dr Morrison came in. We'd passed his car outside a house where a woman I knew was having trouble with a gall stone. On the whole I would prefer the baby. At least you have something to show for your pains.

I stayed in the hospital six days, in spite of what Dr Morrison ordered. On the morning of the sixth day Agnes came in.

"Joan," she said, "I do hate to worry you, but I think you must know. That wretched feckless girl is taking the children round the shops and leaving them outside in the snow for hours while she flirts with the shop boys. I don't know how Rosemary is - she's always in the pram when I see them, but Christopher has a dreadful cough and he's not at all well. I'd say myself he's got bronchitis."

She went home, leaving me absolutely churned up. A few minutes later Matron came in, doing her rounds. I said,

"Matron, I'll have to get home: one of the children is sick, and I'm worried about the little one. Francis has to be away so much of the time on vacation courses for his degree, he can't oversee what's going on. I'll have to go home."

"Dr Morrison won't be pleased. He said you're to have a good rest."

"How can I, when things are going wrong at home? Damn and blast that slut of a girl. Look, Matron, I'll discharge myself. Will you ring Forbes Phillips and ask him to pick me up? Tell Dr Morrison not to be angry; I've no option."

Forbes picked me up and decanted me and the small scrap that was David at the house. As I got out of the car, I saw Christopher, standing in the snow. I thought, "He'll run to me and grab me round the knees and I'll hug him." But he didn't run to me. I called and he turned and toiled slowly through the snow, and when he reached me he laid his head against my legs, and whispered, "Oh, Mummie."

Forbes brought my bag inside for me; I carried David, and held Christopher by the hand. In the nursery I laid David in the waiting cot.

"Where's Rosemary?"

"Morag took her out."

I took his snow suit and his boots off. He was burning hot, and the cough shook his whole small body. I undressed him and put him into bed.

With that, the door burst open and Dr Morrison appeared in a royal rage.

"Who told you that you could leave hospital? What right had you to leave? I told you you needed the rest."

"Oh, please," I said, "Don't scold me. Just come here and look at Christopher. He's running a hell of a temperature. Agnes says that damn girl has had him standing about in the snow for hours while she flirts with the village boys."

He confirmed that Christopher was sick, very sick, with bronchitis, and announced he would bring me some medicine round himself. And where was Rosemary? I said I didn't know: somewhere round the village. Not to worry, he'd send the girl straight back with her.

Rosemary was a dainty child, dainty in her habits. When I went into hospital she was thirteen months old, clean and drinking out of her mug. When the girl brought her home I changed her nappy. She was caked with dried faeces. Her nappies hadn't been changed since Francis did it before leaving in the morning, and the same nappies had been left on her till he returned. Gently I bathed her clean, and she cried with pain. She was completely raw.

The next morning when Morag came, I paid her what I owed her: I wish I could have paid her for the pain and sickness her idleness had caused - and told her that was the end. I never saw her again. Now I should have to do everything myself, but at least I would know that the children were properly cared for.

Christopher took some time to recover from that bad attack of bronchitis, and it seemed to leave him with a slight chest weakness. The next year he had another attack, but we were able to catch it in time. Rosemary healed up well, but how unnecessary all that had been.

Some time after I had finished with Morag somebody in the village told me of her background. The mother was presumably a widow, with the two daughters, Morag and the other girl. The mother had an elderly lodger who slept with the mother or either sister, as the fancy took him. He was known in the village as the Grey Stallion. The elder girl had already had two children by him and now the younger, Morag, was pregnant by him. I wished with all my heart we had never come across the family. If only somebody had thought to say, "Don't take her!"

CHAPTER 23

PROBLEMS AND SOLUTIONS

The start of the New Year was not particularly brilliant for us. My early return from hospital and the mass of troubles I found waiting for me resulted in my being unable to feed David, the tiny new baby. Too much worry, too much work, were having an effect on him that might well have cost his life. I consulted Mr McKay the chemist, and he suggested several replacement foods, but nothing suited the baby, and soon it became apparent even to my unwilling eyes, that instead of making progress he was slipping back.

Dr Morrison summed it all up when he said,

"You know, Joan, there are some tiny babies that never get their feet on the road. There's nothing to be done. Just remember this."

I battled on, doing everything I could think of to help him, to get him to take nourishment. He was hungry, I knew, yet when he had fed, his poor little legs jerked up into his tummy and he screamed with pain. Something in the feeds didn't agree with him, but what was it?

One evening when he was three months old he lay on my lap screaming, and I noticed that his legs, jerking up and down like two little pistons, were just as big round as my thumb. A sudden wave of rebellion rose up in me: we would save him, we could not let him die. The next day Francis brought me home a copy of Truby King's baby book, and in it I found an analysis of breast milk. I took it round to Mr McKay, and we figured out the nearest we could get to it. It needed all sorts of things which I can't remember now, but I bought all the ingredients I could and went home to concoct my own approximation of breast milk. I also carried home with me as a long loan, Mr McKay's baby scales, the sort with a nice warm padded

226

basket for the baby to lie in. Back home I put the scales in the nursery. Then I went to the kitchen, laid out all the ingredients I had bought and made up the new feed. For the one ingredient I'd been unable to buy, a form of sugar, I substituted clover honey. I changed him, settled him on my lap and began to feed him; he took it eagerly. I waited in dread for the colic and screams that inevitably followed each feed, but David gave a loud burp and a gummy smile: there were no screams. I waited half an hour: he had fallen asleep. I could hardly believe it.

Three hours later his next feed was the same. That evening I laid him on the scales and incredulously I saw that he had gained half an ounce, the first gain for weeks. And so it went on. Never again did we have to endure the sight of him struggling in pain, and the feed ejected in great lumps. Every day I weighed him, and every day the scales showed a small gain. It was wonderful.

In July I took Mr McKay's baby scales back to him: we had no more need of them.

It was while I was still struggling with David's digestive problems and Francis was preparing for his final exams that Rosalind, his mother, decided to visit us. We suggested that she should put off her visit by a few weeks till things had settled down and we could make her more welcome, but apparently she could not do so, and she found a very preoccupied son and daughter-in-law. We couldn't put her up, but found a neighbour who often had paying guests in the summer, and Rosalind slept there and had breakfast there. She was comfortable, and they made her welcome for our sakes. I can't say her visit was a huge success: it wasn't, and I think we were all relieved when it came to an end.

Looking back rather sadly, I would say that Rosalind had very little appreciation of the pressures Francis was enduring with his studies and the bee business. I, too, was under tremendous pressure with two small children and a sick baby, and with no help now that Morag had gone her unlamented way.   Rosalind had never had to cope with more than one child, and I myself had very little understanding of her unfortunate ability to alienate people, and of her resulting essential loneliness.   Poor Rosalind; it was a long time before I saw her again, and by then much had happened.

*   *   *

David was putting on weight and had turned at last into a happy baby, still small, but with a proper appetite. He was a real advertisement for Truby King's analysis of human milk and for honey.   Rosemary was as gentle and happy as ever, and Christopher was now a cheerful, mischievous child.   When I went into Mrs McLeod's wee shop to get some socks for the children, she told me that the day before while I was busy in another shop, he had dashed in, struck a dramatic attitude, and pointed at something on the floor, and shouted,

"Yon's a moose!"

"Really, Mrs Smith," she said, "I didn't know whether to laugh at him speaking the Buchan or jump on the counter."

"What did you do?" I asked.

"I laughed," she said, "and so did he, and he raced out of the shop.   The saucy wee thing."

The year moved on: spring came at last, the snow melted into sludge, warm winds blew and the sludge and mud vanished.   The earth, newly exposed after its long winter sleep, suddenly was covered with the fresh green of growing things, the days grew longer, Francis came home in the light at first and then in full sunshine.   Summer was here, long sunny days, warmth and flowers and fruit, all sorts of things I'd forgotten about in the long dark winter.

The children flourished; Christopher spent hours on his tiny tricycle, Rosemary was toddling and David, our only dark Bardwell child, put on weight till he was almost chubby. Life was good.

Next to us in this little enclave lived the Adams. Benjy had returned from the hell of the Burma Railway and looked as though it had never happened, though he still had nightmares. He had picked up the threads of pre-war life, married Heather and was back running his chemist shop in Ballater. He and Heather had one little girl, Katie, a charming little thing a year older than Christopher and with a cap of crisp red curls. She was just a year and a half old the first time we spent an evening with them. The little soul trotted out from her bed and climbed up on her father's lap. She snuggled down, and he asked,

"And who are you?"

"I'm Daddy's wee blether" she said, and I nearly dropped in my tracks.

It was some six months later, and the weather still warm, when one evening, as I was bathing the babies, this little person walked in. I had all three children in the bath, Christopher at one end, then Rosemary, and at the other end, a rather wobbly David, in the big bath with them for the first time. Just as she came in I realised I had left his nightie behind in the bedroom. I stood up, took two steps to the door, three more into the nursery, picked up the nightie, and as I turned back to the bathroom, Daddy's Wee Blether shut the bathroom door and turned the catch which locked it. I was shut out. I went cold.

"Open the door, dear," I said as calmly as I could. "Let me in."

"Can't." she said. And lost interest. And David, balanced so precariously in the bath? My God, if he tipped over, would Christopher understand and lift him up? Could he? Rosemary couldn't, I knew that.

I tried, oh, how I tried, increasingly frantic, to get Katie to open the door, but she was busy splashing the children with bath water. Where was Heather? But what could she do? Nobody could open that door from the outside.

Then I had an inspiration. I flew over the road to Agnes Reid's house and banged on the door.

"Quick, Agnes, is Wee Teddie home yet? Katie's locked the bathroom door and all the children are in the bath and I can't get in. David's in the bath, and it's the first time I've put him in with the others. I'm scared he'll fall over in the water. Could Wee Teddie climb in through the little push-out window at the top of the big window and open the door?"

Wee Teddie, Agnes and I ran back. Rosemary was crying, so was Katie. Mixed sobs of "I want my Mummie" wafted out through that little partly opened window. There was no sound at all from David. Oh, my God!

We boosted Wee Teddie up to the window and head first through the little push out; he just managed to slither in. Moments later, having reversed himself on the way down, he clicked open that stupid lock and opened the door. I nearly fell in on top of him.

The three children were still in the bath: they had stopped crying to watch open mouthed Wee Teddie's descent. Miraculously, David was still upright in the rapidly cooling water.

Katie, wet to the shoulders and still holding Christopher's yellow duck, turned back to the bath and plunged the duck back in. I picked up David and swathed him in a towel.

"Katie," I said, "I think I hear your Mummie calling." So she went - with duck.

*   *   *

I don't remember who it was that made that wretched toy for Christopher. It wasn't as though he needed more toys: by the time he went to bed at night the sitting room floor was so covered with the things that you risked your life answering the door. But that's beside the point: he had it, and he loved it and he wouldn't be separated from it. And what was it? Simply an old cotton reel, the wooden kind, which some kindly donor had chipped all round its edges till it was like a cog wheel. This thing, with an elastic band through its middle and a stub of pencil, used to twist it up tight, gave me one of my more shame-making experiences in a history of many.

Getting the family ready for church was always a tour of strength: you had to do it in the proper order. Get yourself ready first, properly dressed, hair done, collection ready, the lot. Next the youngest, the least mobile. Change him, dress him, lay him back in his cot. Then Rosemary, mobile but not, so far, into mischief, and last of all Christopher: find him, divorce him from what he was up to, clean him up, dress him and corral him until he could be transferred safely into the car. For, yes we had acquired a car, but that's another story.

This particular Sunday - shall I ever forget it? - we were a little late starting out; something had distracted me between finishing Christopher and our all getting into the car. I made sure he had a handkerchief: I should have frisked him, but I didn't. And in the pocket of his small shorts he had that wretched cotton reel.

Off we went to church. He was as good as gold, all the way, almost angelic. We reached Banchory, parked the car and went into church. Banchory church is narrow and very long. It was pretty full but we found room halfway from the front. Francis and I did our usual 'divide and rule' with the children, but how did it come about that Christopher sat at the end of the pew?

All went well until half way through the Mass. David smiled around gummily. Nice elderly ladies smiled at us and our sweet little children, sitting so quietly. All was perfect peace - until Christopher sneezed, reached into his pocket and pulled out his handkerchief. With it out flew this wretched cotton reel, the rubber band fully wound, and it hit that hollow wooden floor with a sound like thunder. Every head turned round, every eye swivelled to the source of the noise, the priest at the altar paused. Time was suspended. Then just as the shock was wearing off and he moved to resume operations, that dam' thing, lying all alone in the middle of the aisle, moved, just one notch, Bang! . . . and then another, Bang! . . and another, Bang! Then in ever increasing speed, it cavorted its foul way, right to the altar steps, Christopher in hot pursuit. It stopped, exhausted, and he picked it up, pocketed it and returned to his loving parents. There was a longish disapproving silence before the service resumed, and all eyes returned to their front.

We left smartly at the end of the Mass.

*   *   *

We needed transport really badly, and all I had was the pram. Francis had bought himself a light motor bike, and in good weather he used it to go to Aberdeen every day. It was a cheaper way of travelling than using the train, although he lost those two hours of undisturbed study. During the weekends and holidays he could ride quickly to the apiary at Fordie or wherever the bees were, and keep an eye on them. He could also do some shopping for me for I had no way of getting about with the children, specially in the winter.

We thought about it and talked about it endlessly, and then, when David was born and there were three small children to be transported, we decided; we must look for a cheap, dependable car.

At last we heard of one which seemed just what we needed. It was a shooting brake, one of those cars, now vanished, with bodies that looked as if they were made of wood. Perhaps they were. It was very roomy and looked to be in good condition. It had belonged to the Aberdeen Police Force. Francis test drove it, was pleased with its performance and bought it. "It's nice to buy a used car from a reputable body," he said, "I don't think we can go far wrong with a car from the police."

That was a happy day. We both piled in, I with Christopher on my lap and we drove off. I had been stuck in Torphins for so long that it was the greatest treat in the world just to get in and be driven out of the village. The car went like a dream. The only trouble was that as we went round a corner my door flew open and Christopher and I had fallen halfway out before Francis grabbed my coat and hauled me back inside.

He began to teach me to drive:

"It's about time you learned to drive. I mayn't always be around to drive you. You need to be independent."

He decided to give me my first lesson one Sunday morning on the way back from Mass at Aboyne. It didn't seem too difficult to keep on the road, and anyway the road was completely empty of traffic for miles. I thought Francis looked a bit tense, but I was doing fine.

Then the road took a right angle turn to the left and passed under the Aberdeen-Ballater railway. It was a narrow bridge. I took a firm grip of the wheel and headed for the gap. And at that moment the only car for miles appeared, moving fast and right in the middle of the narrow way. My hands froze on the wheel and the car headed straight for him. At the last moment Francis grabbed the wheel and we swerved past. Beyond the bridge he stopped me.

"Move over," he said, "my nerves won't take any more today."

He was very quiet on the way home, and didn't answer when I asked him when I could have my next lesson.

That car, or truck or whatever it was, was a Commer with a mighty body and a big engine. It was a sheer delight, for at least two weeks. Then, in some unaccountable way, it began to develop a thirst for oil. At first neither of us thought much about it: in the Forces we hadn't had much to do with petrol and oil consumption. But the matter became worse and worse: the wretched car seemed to have a positive addiction to oil, and at last we took it round to Forbes Phillips for his expert diagnosis. I said bitterly to Forbes, "I don't know much about cars, but I can't ever remember my father driving up to a petrol station for a pint of petrol and a gallon of oil. Something's got to be done. The dam' thing is taking the food out of the babies' mouths."

Forbes made comforting noises about timing and so on and suggested we came back in the evening; but when we did, he was wearing his most serious expression and I knew before he spoke that things were bad.

"Well, Francis." he said, "I hate to bring bad news, but your car has been doctored by an expert - aye, just doctored up for the sale, and the doctoring's wearing off. The wear on the cylinders is phenomenal."

"I bought it," said Francis, "simply because I trusted the sellers - I bought it from the Aberdeen Police."

"Aye, well," Forbes pulled off his cap and scratched the back of his head, "You ken fine what they say about the folk frae Aberdeen? You can read it in *The Press and Journal* any day, 'Aberdeen taxi crashes: all passengers injured. Fifteen in hospital'"

We were lucky: we sold the monster after giving it a rebore, to a man from Lumphanan who admired the extra strong back axle. He had an enormous family, which filled it up very nicely. He was also a fishmonger and handy with his own car repairs. We watched him drive it away, small hands waving from all the windows, and felt no sorrow at all.

* * *

It was in Francis's last term at University that another anxiety struck us. All his Year had been assured that when they had obtained their degrees, they would more or less automatically join the Forestry Commission.

But now Burma had obtained its independence and its Forest Department would be staffed by Burmese officers. The British expatriate officers would return home and would be taken on by the Forestry Commission. Because of this extra drain on their resources the Commission would be unable to pay the new graduates, almost all ex-service men, the salary they had been promised, which included annual increments for their years of war service. Unmarried officers would probably be able to manage without these increments, but we knew that with our family we would not be able to make ends meet. It was all a great worry.

Towards the end of the final year of the forestry course, Francis and his fellow students went down to the south of England to study the management of the New Forest, with its wide amenity belts alongside the roads, and the plantations of pines which were mainly concealed from view from the public.

The group of undergraduates who went to the New Forest was under the guidance of Professor Steven, the Professor of Forestry, and it was a very worth-while course. But for Francis the most interesting occurrence took place in a pub, 'The Silent Woman', where they had all gone for lunch. It was there that their group was joined by Mr Perry, the Director of Recruitment for the Colonial Office, who, with the Forest Advisor, was having informal interviews with those students who had applied to join the Colonial Forest Service.

Francis was talking with some of his friends, a mug of beer in one hand and bread and cheese in the other, when Mr Perry noticed him and asked Professor Steven,

"What about that chap over there?"

"Oh," said the professor, "He's been paying his way through university keeping bees; he's interested in doing bee research."

"Bees!" said the Director of Recruitment, "He's just the man we want. We've been looking for a graduate to do bees for a long time."

And he left the professor and made his way through the crowd. He touched Francis on the shoulder, and when he turned round, said,

"Would you like to do bees in Tanganyika?" Francis, mindful of the fact that Forest Officers on first appointment in the Colonial Service had always been expected to do their first three-year tour alone, leaving their families behind, said,

"I have a wife and three children."

"Oh, that's all right, you can take them with you."

"In that case I'd like to hear more about it."

Term finished at Aberdeen: it was the end of Francis's degree course. Now all we had to do was to wait for the exam results, and that wasn't easy. Luckily, we both had plenty to do to keep our minds off things, but eventually the results came through: he had passed, and in a few days would graduate as a Bachelor of Science (Forestry).

Now the question of this job in Tanganyika came up again. We didn't want to leave Scotland, or England. We just wanted to stay put, but the plain truth was that the salary the UK Forestry Commission could offer us was just not enough, and the pay in Tanganyika, at least on paper, was twice as much. Further, in Tanganyika, I would be able to get help in looking after the children and running the household.

Francis accepted the Tanganyika job. And that is how we went to Africa. But before we left Torphins, there were many sadnesses, particularly uprooting ourselves from the village where our roots had sunk so deeply, saying goodbye to so many people whose lives had become interwoven with our own, selling most of our three-year-old furniture, even the Dunkley Duchess pram which was my pride and joy, and worst of all, selling Fordie Apiaries, Francis's own creation.

We had to equip ourselves for living in Africa and that meant a journey to London to visit the overseas outfitters at the end of September. While on the Underground railway in London, a young woman sitting near us showed signs of chicken pox, and I caught it. Back in Torphins, we had to wait until each of the children developed the symptoms and could be officially cleared of infection. Meantime our air tickets to Dar es Salaam stood on the mantle piece. We eventually left Torphins on the 26th November 1949. I still have the one way ticket from Torphins to Kings Cross.

It is clear that that was of far greater significance to me than General Eisenhower's Citation which never reappeared. When I wrote to the Pentagon some years later to ask if I could have a copy, and had sent a reminder every twelve months for three years, they eventually informed me that they had lost the 1945 file.

GLOSSARY

A A	Anti-aircraft (Ack-Ack)
AB64	Army Book No. 64; Soldier's pay book and identity
ATS	Auxiliary Territorial Service
BBC	British Broadcasting Corporation
CO	Commanding Officer of a regiment or battalion
DC3	A highly versatile transport aircraft known as 'Dakota'
D-Day	6th June 1944, Landings in Normandy
DP	Displaced person
GI	American enlisted man
HMT	His Majesty's Troopship
LDV	Local Defence Volunteers
MO	Medical Officer
NAAFI	Navy, Army and Air Force Institute;
NCO	Non-commissioned Officer
PX	Post Exchange; American form of NAAFI
PYTHON	Scheme to repatriate veteran troops from abroad
RA	Royal Artillery
RAF	Royal Air Force
RN	Royal Navy
RSM	Regimental Sergeant-major, Warrant Officer Class I
RTO	Railway Transport Officer
SHAEF	Supreme Headquarters Allied Expeditionary Force
UNRRA	United Nations Relief and Rehabilitation Administration
US	United States
VAD	Voluntary Aid Detachment
VD	Venereal disease
VE-Day	8th May 1945, end of the war in Europe
WAC	American Women's Army Corps
WRNS	Women's Royal Naval Service (Wrens)

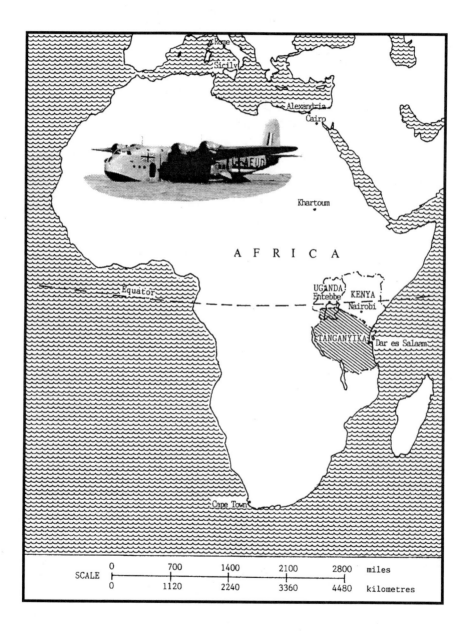

Rome
Sicily
Alexandria
Cairo
Khartoum

A F R I C A

Equator

UGANDA
Entebbe
KENYA
Nairobi
TANGANYIKA
Dar es Salaam

Cape Town

SCALE	0	700	1400	2100	2800	miles
	0	1120	2240	3360	4480	kilometres

BOOKS BY THE SAME AUTHOR

A PATCH OF AFRICA
ISBN 0 9587538 1 4
vii + 232 pages, two maps, 16 photographs

HEART OF AFRICA
ISBN 0 9587538 4 9
x + 202 pages, one map, 32 photographs

Vivid poignant stories of life in Tanganyika in the 1950s and early 1960s. Beautiful, well rounded volumes of tales of a family attuned to up-country life. Joan opens the door on the affection and respect which existed between many Europeans and Africans.

In common with 90 per cent of all people who spend significant parts of their lives in Africa, Joan Smith lost her heart to the country where she lived for more than 12 years - Tanganyika as it was then. *Heart of Africa*, her second book of tales of that period, makes enjoyable reading. They are not tales of wild adventure - just those of family adventure in the bush, of a gentler Africa than that featuring in the news bulletins of today. There's also the mystery of the missing German gold bullion and the clues she found. Is it still lying undiscovered in Tabora where the fleeing German officials hid it? Cunningly she's left this intriguing yarn until the 29th chapter of this 30-chapter paperback. It's a book to pick up and savour chapter by chapter.

John Collier, formerly of *The East African Standard*